13 LESSON  LEADERS

BY

JEAN JUNIOR GABY DORALUS

DEDICATION

To my lovely wife, Ruthnie Doralus, and my two gorgeous children, Kenan Junior Doralus, and Eunice Grace Doralus.

TABLE OF CONTENTS

ACKNOWLEDGMENT

First, I want to thank the Almighty God for giving me this Holy Spirit inspired vision. And also for choosing me by His grace as a channel to bring light to this generation by using the exemplary leadership lifestyle of Jesus Christ and His disciples.

Furthermore, I want to thank Pastor Gregory Toussaint for his sound teachings that has help me to remain steadfast in my service to Lord Jesus Christ. Much more, for inspiring me through His powerful Christian leadership skills.

Also, I want to thank an amazing entrepreneur, Johnson Napoleon, who also motivated me by his strong story and his advice on social media about entrepreneurship.

Finally, I feel a deep sense of gratitude to a prolific writer, Osagiede Ofure, for her tireless commitment, diligent collaboration and advice.

I remain eternally grateful. God bless you all.

INTRODUCTION

Have you ever seen soldiers in action? Was it the navy seals you saw? Or the Marines? Maybe you saw the Black Ops soldiers? What about a special agent in combat? Well, no matter what kind of military officer you've seen in action, one thing comes to mind when you see the excellence of their skill. Instinctively, you know that someone who can engage an enemy like these guys didn't wake up that way. Of course not! It would have taken years of grueling training and painful discipline. Yes, the making of these extraordinary men and women would have required much sacrifice and focus. I believe you might gasp in terror when you realize what makes a soldier.

Likewise, the making of a leader requires much sacrifice and endurance. You probably won't climb mountains or scale great heights. Yet if you want to be a great leader there are prices to pay, processes to go through and knowledge to acquire. Consider this: how many times have you seen a great leader, and you couldn't stop staring in admiration? I've been there too! But most times we forget about what made that leader. More often than not, we shy away from talking about a soldier's scars and a leader's losses.

At this point, are you still anxious to be a great leader? Do you want to make a tremendous impact on your world? Do you want to be the everlasting muse of generations? Does the thought of becoming a great leader someday thrill you? If yes, then you're holding the right book.

This book contains a comprehensive analysis and guidance on how to be a great leader who wields quality influence. So, accept my hearty felicitations for having this book in your hands. It signifies that you are passionate about the subject of leadership. And that you are ready to pay the price no matter how huge it may be. You are ready to be made!

Lao Tsu, an ancient Chinese philosopher, once said, "The journey of a thousand miles begins with a step." Yes, your transformation into a great leader began the moment you picked up this book. And just by taking this adventurous journey on leadership with me, I can say you are halfway already.

Leadership was the sole reason for the massacre of 20 million people in 1939. Yes! Leadership. Bad leadership, for that matter. Someone once said, there are three essential things that every nation needs. In essence, the first is leadership; the second is leadership, and the third is leadership. And that's how important effective leadership is to humanity.

This book is deliberately written to capture the essentials of great leadership. And also, teach you how well you can utilize them to function effectively as a great leader regardless of your environment, personality, or background.

The first thing I would like to point your attention to is that we all are leaders. Or should I say everyone has the seed of leadership in them? Leadership occurs at various levels, from a family man to a class captain to a school principal and up to a chief executive officer of a multinational company. All that is left for you is to nurse and nurture that seed until it becomes a blooming sheltering tree for many others.

In his book, John C. Maxwell asserted, 'Leadership is influence; nothing more, nothing less.' While that is true, we must examine the source of the influence; as influence can either be positive or negative. In this book, we take cues from past successful leaders to investigate the mystery behind leadership.

Subjective leadership

Warren Bennis opined that *"the point is not to become a leader. The point to become yourself."* John C. Maxwell also said that a true leader knows the way, goes the way and shows the way. So in this book, you are going to learn how human beings are the first social species and that as we interact with people, we become receptive to their opinions. Eventually, as time goes on, this influences the kind of person we become. And that explains why the journey to authentic leadership starts with knowing your identity. How do you know which direction to go when you're entirely oblivious to your current location? A great leader furnishes his strengths and then converts his weaknesses to strengths. To wield influence, he must be void of egotism and full of virtues; sacrificial, loving, and insightful. An emotionally imbalanced leader will always dance to the tune of well-wishers and ill-wishers alike. Someone who cannot control himself, how can he lead others? Good listening skills, empathy, adept communication skills and other inherent traits are all characteristic of a great and influential leader.

Objective leadership

Are you having challenges with building healthy relationships with your followers? Does the thought of standing before and addressing your subjects scare you? No. It doesn't have to be. Based on observed environmental facts and situations, a great leader must be able to take cues and decisions as regards how to steer his leadership boat. You will learn how to be a great leader in both good and bad times; amidst both friendly and hostile people. Using given external factors to one's advantage is a skill that a great leader must master.

How do you define a leader who is deaf to the opinions of others? Ken Blanchard said, none of us is as smart as all of us. Teamwork and collaborative skills are quite vital in the quest for acquiring leadership qualities. No one is an island of knowledge. Don't be like King Saul who cringes at the face of a giant when he has a small giant slayer back at home. Everybody needs somebody. Little wonder the bible says, two are better than one for they have a good reward for their labor. In other word, Together, Everyone Achieves More (TEAM).

Ultimate Leadership Style

Leadership examples used in this book range from contemporary figures to ancient luminaries to biblical exemplar. However, Jesus Christ, being our example of the ultimate and perfect leader, serves as our standard throughout this book.

But not so with you. Rather, let the greatest among you become as the youngest, and the leader as one who serves. - Luke 22:26

For the believer, leadership starts with being a servant. This was evident in the life of Christ as washed the feet of his disciples in John

13. Even if you are not a leader in your family, church or home, you sure are called to lead others to Christ. Christ has left us a perfect example that we should walk therein.

Knowing fully well that effective leadership is critical to the survival of humanity itself, shall we them fold our arms and remain bank and vehicles of bad influence? I hope you are now bearing the responsibility to dive deep into this leadership course with me with full assurance that consequently you will become the kind of leader you have always wanted to be; particularly a great leader that is fashioned after Christ.

LESSON 1

GOOD COMMUNICATION SKILLS

"The biggest problem in communication is an illusion that it has taken place."

George Bernard Shaw

J ohn C. Maxwell said, "Leadership is not about titles, positions, or flow charts. It's about one life influencing another." In other words, the passion for helping others realize their dreams is the driving force of a true leader.

Indeed, leadership is about mobilizing and motivating people to commit to a goal with all their heart and strength. As a result, a leader's vision is fueled, not only by passion but also by sustained influence. However, you cannot be influential without effective communication.

Therefore, communication is to leadership what gasoline is to an automobile. It boosts progress, keeps a team on top momentum, and headed in the right direction. Indeed, a good leader is passionate about his vision, but a great leader can effectively transfer that passion to his team.

Picture a huge lighted candle among thousands of wet candles in a dark tunnel. Although there's a flicker of light in the tunnel, it can't be shared among the other candles. Instead, it's in danger of being put out. So is a vision with passion, without proper communication.

Think about this. Do you want a bright tunnel or a dark misty path to nowhere? If you choose the first, then you need to sharpen your communication skills to kindle passion in the heart of your followers. Doing so will make pursuing your vision more productive and successful.

If you are a team leader of an organization (religious or social), you will agree with me that managing a team could be overwhelming sometimes. Everybody may not always be on the same page with you, and this may cause some form of exhaustion. It could make you doubt your influence over the people you are leading.

Have you ever wondered why leadership seems so difficult? Would you like to step up on those behaviors that underpin leadership effectiveness? If yes, then this lesson is for you. It is time to learn the art of effective communication and discover the power of influence and connection in leadership. You may say, "I'm not a leader." However, if you're a person of influence, you're automatically a leader. Perhaps, you guide people with your actions, and they listen to what you say. Or, maybe you're responsible for someone and exercise a level of authority. If you fit into any of these descriptions, then consider yourself a leader.

Also, most times, when you talk to someone, you get to influence him or her in one way or another. Hence, someone's life took a turn, either for better or for worse because of you. You influenced them to take action. Thus, you are a leader, an influencer. And the earlier you accept this, the better. On the other hand, the more you deny, ignore, or reject your leadership identity, responsibility, and reality, the more careless, less significant, or even harmful you become.

You need to accept who you are and embrace the call to leadership. On the other hand, you may say I'm a leader, but not a communicator. Well, that's not only untrue; it's impossible! Because all leaders are communicators.

Nonetheless, not every leader is an excellent communicator. Yet, just as Ralph Waldo Emerson said, "All great speakers were bad speakers at first." So, it doesn't matter if you're a terrible communicator, you can develop the skill. Without effective communication, a leader cannot plant seeds of intense desire and passion in the hearts of his followers.

Do you know what this means? It means that to succeed as a leader, you must be an excellent communicator! Whether by the words you say or the things you do, you must connect with people to gain their trust and influence their actions.

Leadership is about driving ideas that are understood, accepted, and supported by loyal team members or followers. For instance, our body cannot function without high-level and constant communication that takes place along the nerve pathways. Your body operates under the influence or leadership of your brain. Nervous activities are ever-present to help coordinate motion, direction, and function of your body. Not to mention the harmonious mental activities and neurotransmission of signals, which are proofs of communication in the body.

Today, the business world, the political sphere, and the social landscape require effective communication for any success and survival. Obviously, the complexity of our society demands clear, smooth, and effective communication to navigate various challenges of leadership at diverse levels.

Over time, leadership experts, have linked problems in leadership to poor listening and communicating skills. Many leaders tend to talk over their employees or followers. Communication is said to be effective only when there is a mutual understanding. So, where the receiver cannot decode the message, there is no communication. Also, there's a significant lack of information flow, lack of more profound meaning and higher purpose among followers. It's time to do something about these things.

Furthermore, a leader is a voice of hope and a force of change. I believe that you are a leader because the seed of leadership is in you. You are a voice of hope and an agent of transformation in your world.

Nevertheless, your success or failure as a leader hinges on your ability to communicate your vision and engage your followers effectively. The world's greatest leaders are men and women who could communicate hope, inspire trust and confidence, and mobilize support through their effective communication.

Without this, it is impossible to influence others. Admittedly, it takes more than good ideas to change the world. It takes having people inspired by one compelling personality with one big idea.

WORDS CAN CHANGE THE WORLD

"You can have brilliant ideas, but if you can't get them across,

your ideas won't get you anywhere."

- Lee Iacocca

Verbal communication remains the most potent form of communication. The simple reason is this: **words are powerful!** Even though a picture is worth more than a thousand words and actions speaks louder than words; yet, Death and life are in the power of the tongue.

The Bible reveals that Jesus is the **Word of God!** John said, "in the beginning, was the word, the world was made by the word and NOTHING was made without the Word." Everything started and will end with words. Also, all things will rise and fall by words. Words can pierce deep into the heart and soul of man. It's essential that leaders know how to choose their words rightly. In other words, every leader needs to adopt strategies to connect and powerfully share their vision.

For instance, consider Jesus. His kind of leadership was revolutionary, and the Jewish elders desired to snare Him in His own words.

One day, they brought a matter before Him to judge. Some men had caught a woman in adultery, and according to the Law of Moses, it was a crime punishable by death. The men who wanted to carry out this "righteous judgment"—stone her to death--had surrounded this woman like a pack of angry wolves. They wielded their stones in "holy" anger and were just waiting for Jesus to give the word. But guess what?

Jesus was ready! His words were piercing and direct, effectively communicating His mind to His audience. Jesus said, "He that is without sin should cast the first stone." And with just a few words, He had condemned them all of the same crime and had shown them how unfair they were. He struck their conscience and influenced their actions. Do you know what happened next? They hit the road! Each one of them left the poor woman alone.

Think about what Jesus's words did and reflect on the tremendous power you wield. Your words form ideas and thought that become strongholds in the mind of your listeners. Do you realize that you can trace your actions to words you've heard? Have you ever done something because a friend advised or suggested that you should? You must have acted in response to someone's compliments or criticism.

Certainly, words inspire, motivate, control, and influence people; learn to use it! Words are the most potent weapons great leaders use. Words matter! You may be reading this book because you have heard talks on the importance of leadership and the power of knowledge. I hope to influence you with the words I'm writing, because you are an influencer, a leader, and an agent of positive change!

In the gospels, Jesus held 5,000 people spellbound in the wilderness for several days. They were so into His teaching they didn't think about food. Can you imagine that? How excellent were His words? Scriptures also reveal that when Jesus taught in the temple, people gasped at the authority that came with His words.

During His earthly ministry, the Lord Jesus was a leader who understood the value of communication skills. A time came when some of His disciples deserted Him. Because of this, Jesus asked Peter if he was also going to leave. Peter responded by saying he couldn't leave because only Jesus had the **WORDS OF LIFE.** .Jesus spoke life-giving words; his disciples would not trade it for anything else. He retained their loyalty and commitment to the vision by authoritative words and actions!

PAUL: THE STRATEGIC COMMUNICATOR AND GREAT INFLUENCER

I'm about to let you in on a Bible Character widely regarded as the next most influential person to Jesus Christ. His name is Apostle Paul- the great influencer. The secret of his success in leadership isn't arithmetic or quantum physics. It was effective communication. Can you say the same about yourself?

Do you want to engrave your name on the sands of time? Do you want an influence that can outlast your generation into the next? Of course, you do, there's a desire for greatness in all of us. Apostle Paul was a man like you and I. Learn about the man that started, grew, and led many churches in the first century. His achievements towered that of Jesus' 12 disciples. And of the 27 books of the New Testament, 13 were attributed to Paul. He wrote epistles and letters that formed about half of the New Testament Bible.

One thing you must note about Paul is that his speech influenced. Countless millions of people in a different part of the world would stand to listen and follow Him. He was intimidated and attacked; yet, his influence continued to grow all over the Christian world.

Even today, Apostle Paul is still the one of the most influential Christian leaders. So what can we learn about this great leader? Well, one thing is clear about Paul: he knew the power of choosing the perfect words to either refine or revive hearts. He knew what to say to the King, Slave, Officer, Prison Guard, Philosophers, Educated, Barbarians, Jews, and Gentiles. Paul knew the power of fitly spoken words.

How did Paul demonstrate excellent communication skills?

He always attempted to assess and understand his audience

An incident in Acts chapter 17 showed Paul's communication skills. It happened when his missionary journey took him to Athens, a city of the Greeks, people of great learning and knowledge.

While he was there, Paul saw that the Athenians were idol worshippers. As a result, he desired to preach the Gospel to them. The Bible says, "Paul stood up in front of the city council and said, '**I see that in every way you Athenians are very religious.**

For as I walked through your city and looked at the places where you worship, I found an altar on which is written, To an

Unknown God.' That which you worship, then, even though you do not know it, is what I now proclaim to you."

-Acts 17:22-23

One day, Apostle Paul took the time to stand and to look around an Athenian City council. Before he addressed the people, he assessed who they were, diligently looking for the anchor point. He knew that words are leaches, and they must hang on something that won't waste time and effort put into communication.

How often have you seen a leader who just keeps speaking without even taking the time to look carefully? Like a fishing hook and line, a great leader must learn to hook their listeners. Of course, every angler has mastered the place and power of patient-watching. Likewise, when you communicate your heart to people, the right timing is essential. Timing can give life to the message you convey, or annihilate it.

And, before you speak to people, what did you see? Paul said that as he walked around the city of Athens, he found an inscription that caught his attention. An altar to An Unknown God became a perfect talking point, and a means to grab the people's much-needed attention. It was the bait, and the fishes couldn't resist it! They paid attention!

So, what have you found? Have you found an anchor point, or you're just in a hurry to throw in your fishing line and pull it out even if you catch no fish?

Note this. Every great communicator is also a great listener, and an excellent observer. So, next time you want to speak, ask yourself, has my fish swallowed the hook as Im about to pull the line? Don't be in a hurry to talk.

Do you sometimes feel overwhelmed and frustrated because you're unable to secure and retain your listener's attention while you speak on something important to you?

Great leaders have perfected the art of emotional intelligence. They have learned how to feel the pulse of the people. They like to know who you are, what you need to hear, and how to connect with you on a much deeper level. And this is all about expanding and strengthening their influence.

Furthermore, great leaders use words like a leach to draw you into an idea, plan, purpose, or vision. They use words to take you to where you need to be. Also, great leaders don't sweat over this because they carefully apply the leach in strategic places that won't let the influence slip off easily.

Often, great leaders are concerned about what they say because their words are outflows of their passion. Indeed, like a volcanic eruption, words can boil in the heart of a passionate leader. And while having such fiery zeal is good, but greatness lies in self-control- the ability to be sure that you know of your listeners.

He knew how to make necessary mental shifts for what he desired to say.

> *"Although I am free from everyone's expectations, **I have made myself a servant** to all of them to win more people."*

--1Corinthains 9:19 (ISV)

Apostle Paul was a man on a mission. He wanted to win or, better still, influence more people. Paul sought to expand and stretch the impact of his ministry. Yet, he couldn't achieve his goal to change many lives without a cost.

Paul realized that to expand his influence, he needed to consider connecting with people from unfamiliar backgrounds, different races, creeds, and cultures. So, he came up with a superb strategy! I'm sure you would like to know!

Here's Paul's practical guide to effective communication to establish a strategic connection:

"While working with the Jews, I live like a Jew to win them, and even though I am not subject to the Law of Moses, I live as though I were when working with those who are, to win them.

In the same way, **when working with Gentiles, I live like a Gentile,** outside the Jewish Law, in order to win Gentiles. This does not mean that I don't obey God's Law; I am really under Christ's Law.

Among the weak in faith I become weak like one of them, in order to win them".

"So I Become All Things To All People, That I May Save Some Of Them By Whatever Means Are Possible."

-1Corinthians 9:22

Evidently, Paul did all he could to break communication barriers. He reached out to the heart of his hearers. What will you do to influence people? What will you sacrifice to be an effective communicator? When was the last time you communicated with someone, fully understanding who they were and where they came from? Are you always tempted to be critical and judgmental, instead of being empathetic?

It's time to practice intentional awareness when next you reach out to talk with someone you want to influence. Of course, your team members may not tell you the reason they're sometimes out of sync with you. Sometimes, they do things that sabotage the vision of the team, even without knowing it.

The point I'm trying to make is, your followers are usually at the mercy of your ability to communicate effectively. Your ability to connect with them and transmit the same intensity and passion with which you carry your vision. So, if you believe what you say you believe, how far are you willing to go to make someone believe just as you do?

He connected with the Elite and Intellectual

As you grow in your leadership experience, exposure, and influence, you will have great minds, intellectuals, and elite join your team. Moreover, from my experience, I know that leaders always want excellent men and women in their group. You want to influence top professionals and highly efficient people. You want to lead intellectually sound people, people with a knack for wisdom and excellence.

Alexander the Great once said, "I am not afraid of an army of lions led by a sheep; I am afraid of an army of sheep led by a lion." Think about that. To be candid, the passion of the leader is key to the kind of followership he commands. You must always be on top of the communication chain. You must be the lion-size great intellectual, always a step ahead of your team members in terms of an ability to communicate your ideas. Don't be the sheep while your followers are lions. This way, you won't make much progress.

Therefore, the question is not in the caliber of people you are leading but the kind of person you are. Are you an influencer; are you an excellent communicator; would you rise to the occasion and be the leader, even the elite and intellectuals would love to follow trustingly?

Will you allow yourself to be tongue-tied because you are dealing with elites, intellectuals, highly placed men, and women in your team? Have you discovered that leadership is all about leading leaders, influencing influencers, and mobilizing great minds?

You see, having intellectuals in your team bring countless benefits. Besides the fact that you now have people so skillful and efficient, they can make things happen for you pretty quickly. What about Apostle Paul; how did he manage communication and influence with people at the top level in the society?

The truth is when Paul met the Philosophers of Athens; he automatically knew that Athenians were interested in knowledge. They spent their time in nothing else but in revealing or learning new things. These intellectuals brought Paul to the Areopagus, which was the aristocratic council of Athens.

Again, what would you have done if this were YOU? Have you built your mental capacity and communication skills to where you can engage people at all levels of learning and wisdom?

You see, Paul was different! He communicated the good news even in Areopagus- their hall of wisdom. Of course, Paul didn't use the same words he would have with the Jews.

Interestingly, he revealed Christ by quoting Greek philosophy, **"FOR IN HIM WE LIVE, AND MOVE, AND HAVE OUR BEING;** as certain also of your own **POETS** have said."

Indeed, Apostle Paul had a knack for a personal connection to enhance communication with his audience. He intelligently took something that would resonate with his listeners and leveraged on it in a way he engraved his message and personality in people's hearts and minds.

On another occasion, there was Apostle Paul before three great people. A King, a Queen, and a Roman Governor.

King Agrippa; Queen Bernice came to visit Governor Festus. Paul was in the Governor's custody for a long time with no real progress towards freedom. Then, Apostle Paul, being a Roman citizen and self-made advocate, appealed to Caesar in Rome.

However, there was a problem. Governor Festus needed a tag line to state the crime or allegation against Paul. In this case, the Governor sought the wisdom of King Agrippa and Queen Bernice, to know what to write against the accused- Apostle Paul.

Listen to Governor Festus, and you will feel the limitation of the lack of right words. Festus said,

"...it seems unreasonable to me to send a prisoner without clearly indicating the charges against him."

Act 25:27

When a leader cannot rightly use words to express himself, he immediately appears unreasonable, complicated, and even confused. Nothing devalues leadership than poor communication! No wonder Simon Sinek said, "Great leaders communicate and great communicators lead." Notice Agrippa's shift of attention from Festus. Why was that? Festus had no words. He neglected Festus and faced Paul to hear him out.

"Agrippa said to Paul, 'You have permission to speak on your own behalf.' Paul stretched out his hand and defended himself as follows:"

Act 26:1

Back to our story, The King and the Governor agreed to summon Paul and listen to what he had to say. Paul spoke so powerfully and communicated so expertly that King Agrippa said to Paul:

"...A Little More And You Will Be Making Me A Christian!"

Act 26:28

Can you believe that? Paul was so persuasive with words that He almost won the heart of those intellectuals to Christ.

By the way, you need to read the whole book of Acts, chapter 25, to understand the background to this story. And read Acts chapter 26 to grasp the wisdom of Paul's defense, paying attention to how he articulated his story powerfully and convincingly. These were words of a prisoner for the Gospel, but it held a King, a Queen, a Governor, and their entourage spellbound.

Finally, Paul responded to King Agrippa's comment, and I want you to consider the power in his response. He said,

"Whether a short time or a long time," paul answered, "my prayer to god is that you and all the rest of you who are listening to me today might become what i am—except, of course, for these chains!"

Act 26:29

Now, you may be wondering why we're talking so elaborately about Apostle Paul. You may be asking, what's the leadership in sharing the Gospel? Why's Paul a great communicator, leading influencer, and an influential leader? The answer to these questions is in Acts 26, verses 29:

"BECOME AS I AM!"

So, what's the point, purpose, and essence of leadership? It's about influencing people. And transforming them to **becoming like you**

are. I mean, they can do as you do, feel the same way you feel, take steps the way you would, be responsible for the things that matter to the team, and follow carefully in your footsteps in pursuit of a greater good?

Indeed, Apostle Paul was a significant influencer. The three nobles did this just after Paul spoke to them:

"And the king and the ruler and Bernice and those who were seated with them got up; And when they had gone away, they said to one another, This man has done nothing which might give cause for death or prison. And Agrippa said to Festus, This man might have been made free, if he had not put his cause before Caesar."

Act 26: 30-32

Paul spoke his way into people's hearts. He was a great leader! Period and Simple!

LEADING THROUGH WORDS

The threshold of history holds the records of the greatest leaders the world has ever known--Men and women, who influenced cultures and societies by their ability to communicate through words. Most of these great leaders were orators. Able to wield words as good swords. And men revered their words. They led revolutions, started and ended wars, transformed lives, and commanded followership. They led through the power words.

MOSES: THE MAN WHO PERSUADED GOD

What about Moses? One of the most exceptional leaders in Israel. He was a man with excellent communication skills. The Bible records that he was mighty in words and deeds (Acts 7:22).

But the most remarkable thing about this leader's communication skills was that he could convince not only men but also God.

Back when Israel newly found freedom from the Egyptians, Moses led them towards the Promised Land. The people of Israel were a tough bunch to lead and always grumbled against God and Moses. Not too long after they left Egypt, the Israelites sinned against God. They made for themselves a gold statue and worshipped it.

When God saw this, He desired to destroy them and raise a holy generation from Moses' lineage, but Moses swooped into action. He was ready to intercede for his people, and he negotiated their pardon with God so efficiently. This incident is in Exodus chapter 32.

Moses said something that even God could not override or overlook. Moses asked God to have mercy, and God changed His mind. The statement was the game changer!

Moses said that if God destroyed the Israelites, the Egyptians would hear it and say, "He had brought them out of Egypt to destroy them because it was impossible for him to bring the people to the Land that He promised." (Number 14:13)

He reminded God of His covenant with the people of Israel. Moses convinced God by putting his oratory skills to good use. God listened to Moses and withdrew his plan to destroy the entire nation of Israel. Without and influencer and communicator like Moses, an entire nation would have perished! As a leader, can your words save someone's life?

HITLER: THE MAN WHO WIELDED THE WEAPON OF WORDS

A wise man once said, "It's neither the good nor the bad power that dominates a realm, but it's surely the higher power that rules!" Edmund Burke said, "The ONLY thing necessary for the triumph of evil is for good men to do NOTHING!"

How long will you relegate the power of leadership, responsibility, and communication in your sphere of influence? The truth is, nature abhors a vacuum. It means the space you don't fill will be taken and forcefully occupied by another. The only concern is, who are the people allowed to take over? Are we doing all we can to keep society safe by rising to leadership by building all the necessary skills?

A BAD example of an excellent communicator, influencer, and leader was Adolf Hitler. Although he is a negative figure in history because of his atrocities against humanity and bad policies, he was excellent at influencing people to do what he wanted. And I want to show you a few things about his passion for leadership through influence and effective communication.

Check this out: History has it that Hitler delivered over 5,000 speeches in his lifetime. His words were very persuasive. He convinced and bewitched his audience into loyalty, which he got in spades.

He's known in history as one of the world's most influential orators. According to Professor Bruce Loebs of Idaho state university, Adolf Hitler learned to become a charismatic speaker and, by this, endeared himself to many people. You see that the journey was not overnight! He went for gold and never stopped until he got what he wanted!

Furthermore, Prof. Bruce said that Hitler commanded such strident followership because he seemed to have the right answers in a time of great economic confusion and distress.

Also, the Nazi Propaganda Minister Joseph Goebbels revealed that Hitler wrote His speeches and edited them several times before delivering it. Wow! This man knew the power of words.

Then, Professor Loebs, speaking about Hitler's speeches, said that "the German leader took public speaking seriously and trusted no one to write his speeches."

Yet again, George Steiner, a man who lived in Germany during Hitler's reign, described his voice as "overwhelmingly powerful and spellbinding." He shared that as a child, he often heard Hitler's voice on the radio, and he said it was "mesmeric."

Furthermore, George stated that it seemed as if Hitler's whole personality reflects in his voice as he spoke.

Now here's the power of practice. John C. Maxwell said, "Tone, inflection, timing, pace, volume-everything you do with your voice communicates something and has the potential to help you connect to or disconnect from others when you speak."

Are you as motivated as Adolf was? Are you willing to master the right tone, inflection, volume, pace, voice, and language that will enhance your ability to communicate?

You see, Hitler's personal photographer, Heinrich Hoffman (who took several photos of his facial expressions and hand gestures), revealed that the German leader rehearsed his speeches in a mirror and had his picture taken. Afterward, Hitler studied the pictures before he had them destroyed.

More so, According to Professor Loebs, Hitler had to work at his presentation because it was half of his message. And he added animation to communicate his words and ideas effectively.

Unfortunately, Adolf Hitler, as the leader of Germany, created his political theory, conquered nations, and influenced the deaths of over 21 million people. He is a symbol of hatred and evil, but history agreed that he led through his oratory power.

"PEN OF A READY WRITER"

One characteristic of an excellent communicator is the ability to know what somebody needs to hear at a particular time. The Bible calls this timely and strategic information, a word in season. Great leaders always know what to say and when to say it. They are never short of words and can still encourage, rebuke, or motivate where necessary.

In fact, their words are full of grace. It can heal the deepest of wounds and calm the most turbulent seas. Isaiah 50:4 says, "The Lord God has given me the tongue of the learned that I should know how to speak a word in season to him that is weary…"

This kind of communication skill is a gift from God. You see, Great leaders are not only great speakers, but they're also always ready to communicate for the good of their subjects or followers.

FINALLY, GREAT LEADERS NEVER DIE

"…by it he being dead yet speaketh"

-Hebrews 11:4

There're great men living legacies even after they died—Men whose legacies live on because of excellence and the power of communication. They are still in the counseling business. They still mentor leaders. They are still the leading voice in this generation. These kinds of leaders remain influential, no matter their age. Their ability to communicate their vision and passion effectively engraved their memories in the hearts of men. The earth picked up the precise articulation of their purpose. Thus, they abide forever.

My friend, believe me, people live on through their words. Not only through their words but also through their life, which is all their ideas, actions, and being. Do you remember an old church hymn that says, "You'll be remembered by what you've done?" These men had excellent communication skills. Even their silence spoke! Today, they can be used as a frame of reference.

Indeed, people die, but their words don't. You can forget names but not the impact of their words. I mean, how can powerful words that changed lives, built nations, and sustained empires be forgotten? Through their utterance, great men painted the future and stamped it on the canvas of time.

Do you want to be a great leader? Great leaders don't die. What I mean is, they live on through their words. Here's why. Because they had effectively communicated their life to another. Don't get trapped in the image that you are nothing more than ordinary. You can step up, and be a remarkably great leader.

LESSON 2

HOME SUPPORT AND RECOGNITION

"For if a man know not how to rule his own house, how shall he take care of the church of God?"

1TIMOTHY 3:5

Before a plant germinates, it is first under the soil, where it is protected, nurtured, and well-fed with good nutrients. When the plant is ready to go into the sunlight, the soil influences it to move out, to break the surface and get ahead.

No true leader emerges without having gone through a series of underground building and nurturing, and then positive influences motivating them to come up to the surface and rise to meet the sun.

A plant that doesn't do well under the ground can't break the surface and come out. Imagine a plant not surrounded by the warm nutrition found in fertile soil. Instead, toxic chemical substances under the ground surround it. Such a plant would be too busy fighting off the negative influences, trying hard to survive the soil that contrives to subdue it, to have the strength to rise.

Similarly, a great leader is first successful at home. He or she must have been able to garner support and influence from his own family members or a pseudo-family. This support is like nutrients to his skills and aspirations. The positive words of affirmation and the practical assistance all combine to make an excellent place for the leader in him to manifest. He can move forward, and when the time comes for such a leader in emerging, the encouragement and optimism all contribute to push him up and into the sunlight.

However, a man who has to fight with negativity in his home, pessimism, and words of doubt, will be so busy trying to shake all these off that he will be too weak or distracted to get on, get ahead, and move along. The influences that the leader can gather from his home base would contribute to or take away from his influence and leadership ability. The home turf is the most significant sphere of influence for a leader to conquer and command followership. It is often also the last.

For many leaders, influences from their background and the atmosphere of their home continue to hold them back. Such a leader could try to excel regardless of his bad history with his family. But, there's no true greatness with unresolved family issues.

Unfortunately, a lot of the leaders who cannot deliver are unaware that several strings hold up a great leader. These strings are from several angles in the leader's support system. To succeed, you must be able to tap into the many reservoirs of positivity and encouragement. These reservoirs are people, and those people make up your support system.

In plants, nutrients are taken in through their roots, and if you have ever observed the roots of a plant, you would know that the root is multiple in each plant. They spread around the tree, and each draws up nutrients that strengthen and nurture the plan. Your support system is like a collection of people, soaking up positivity, and pushing out to you. Without the roots, the plant would die because it would starve. In the same way, without home support, you wouldn't receive the encouragement and nurturing that you need.

On the other hand, with excellent home support, you will find that the leader is motivated and inspired to go higher. Because he has the strength he needs in the group of people who support him. Indeed, you can't give what you don't have.

However, many leaders today ignore this sphere and go on to affect the world. But those who do so never become great leaders, although they may be "good" leaders. Therefore, you are a great leader when your family believes in you enough to follow you. Because naturally, your family members are the most difficult people to lead.

Now, we've established that Jesus was a great leader. I mean, this is undeniable. The Lord Jesus Christ continues to be an unequaled enigma when it comes to the subject of leadership. He did it flawlessly. Yet He said this when he went to His hometown and got a reception that differed from the one He had received abroad:

> *"…A prophet is not without honor, but in his own country, and among his own kin, and in his own house"* **– Mark 6:4**

Wow! Can you look at this? Jesus was talking about Himself as a Prophet, a religious **leader** who speaks for God. He discovered that everybody, except the people He grew up with, believed in Him. Well, Jesus said He wasn't surprised. Such rejection is many leaders, the burden they bear. He was saying that what happened to him was the natural order of things, and it was because of specific reasons, unfounded, as they may seem.

FAMILIARITY KILLS INFLUENCE

What could have been the reason for anyone to doubt such a great teacher and healer? Jesus, who at a young age, had taught teachers in the synagogue, what could it be that would stop people from believing in him? FAMILIARITY!

In verse three of the same chapter, when the people in Jesus' home town heard the words He spoke, they wondered and asked themselves, "Is not this the carpenter, the son of Mary, the brother of James, and Joses, and of Juda and Simon? And are not his sisters here with us?" And the Bible says that they got offended. They must have thought, "We know this kid. I watched him grow up. I saw him in diapers. What makes him think that he can tell us what to do? We know that he did not even attend a good college. He did not have any tutors of high repute. My son studied law, and he is not out here trying to tell us what to do. Who does this carpenter's son, think he is?"

Friend, I don't know if you have ever experienced something similar. Can you relate? Have people rejected your idea, contribution, or leadership because they couldn't see your greatness? They remember your weaknesses and limitations. They remember that you grew up in their neighborhood and that you played out in the backyard buck-naked. Now, you tell them you are a man of authority and expect them to believe in your skills?

Possibly, your extended family contributed to pay your tuition fee. They've all helped you out of their generosity, and here comes this little fella trying to be somebody, acting like he knows better than the rest of them.

One thing made them reject Jesus as a Prophet who worked signs and wonders. It was nothing other than familiarity! They had seen him too often. They felt they knew him too well. The people from Jesus' childhood saw Him as other things.

First, they saw Him as a carpenter. I bet they scoffed at Him. Perhaps, they had seen him picking up nails and gathering wood. In their minds, that was who Jesus was, a carpenter, and maybe not even a good one.

Second, they saw Him as someone they knew all about. They didn't even call Him Jesus. They called Him the son of Mary. In essence, they were saying, "we knew your mother before you were born. After you were born, we were acquainted with you growing up. We know you, kid. Or more politely, we know you, Jesus. We played together on the streets. In fact, you once got your head stuck in a barrel." Has anyone ever made you feel that way? Has someone ever talked to you as though he/she knew you like the palm of their hand? I know all about you, they say.

Peradventure, this is your experience, don't write yourself off. Jesus went through the same thing. And I know you might say, "I thought Jesus was a great leader. His family didn't believe in Him too?" Journey with me further, and I'll show you something thoughtful.

AS JESUS NOT A GREAT LEADER?

Earlier, we saw that being a great leader begins when your family believes in you enough to follow you. And we established that Jesus was a great leader. But surprisingly, the Lord Himself said that "a prophet is not without honor except in his own house." This means he experienced some level of rejection and unbelief from His family.

21

The Bible reveals in John chapter 7 that his brothers didn't believe in him and even mocked him.

It was the time of the Jewish feast of Booths, which took place in Judea. But here was Jesus in Galilee. His brothers said to him, "Depart hence, and go into Judaea, that thy disciples also may see the works that thou doest. For there is no man that doeth anything in secret, and he himself seeketh to be known openly. If thou do these things, shew thyself to the world".

Now at first glance, what Jesus' brothers said sounds like a piece of good advice, but they were mocking him. They asked Him to show himself that everybody will see the works (miracles) He does, and then they said, "…If you do these things". They never believed he was a miracle worker. John 7:5 made it more apparent. It says that for neither did his brethren believe in Him.

So does this mean that Jesus wasn't a great leader? No, it doesn't. First, Jesus didn't have the full support and recognition of His family, but over time he, did.

HOME SUPPORT AND RECOGNITION IS EARNED

Leadership is a journey. And on your journey, you will encounter mountains you need to conquer and add to your sphere of influence. And the family is one of those mountains.

I'm sure you know that respect is like an income; it doesn't just come to you because you need it, it is earned. It is the same with support and recognition from your family. If they ever believe in you as others do, you must earn it.

Therefore, although Jesus made that statement, expressing His regret because of the dishonor He got from His own people, as He continued His journey in leadership, he earned their support and confidence.

For example, do you remember the wedding at Canna in Galilee? Jesus and His mother Mary, were present at the marriage feast, and the wine ran out. Jesus' mother asked Jesus to do something about it. She knew what He was capable of, and she believed in Him. She was too sure of her son that she asked the servants to do whatever Jesus told them to do. Her trust and support were worthy of note.

That was all Jesus needed to get on and embrace his destiny as a leader. He may not have had to earn the support and recognition of the rest of his family and his village. However, he had the trust, belief, encouragement, and complete acknowledgment of his mother to start with. Jesus' mother knew that he would be great and so she continued to be positive and to give him the nutrients he needed to come into the reality of his place as God's Son and the Messiah. Imagine if he had been born to a woman who always talked him down and told him he was born into a carpenter's family and so would never accomplish much.

What about his brothers who didn't believe in Him but ridiculed Him? They, too, later believed in Him and even became Christians. In Acts 1:14, the Bible records that Jesus' mother and His brothers were in the upper room with all the disciples waiting for the promise of the Holy Spirit.

In fact, two of Jesus' brothers, James and Jude, played critical roles in the New Testament. James became the leader of the Church in Jerusalem, and Jude wrote one of the New Testament epistles.

They were not touched supernaturally. On the contrary, Jesus earned the recognition and faith of these people.

GIVE ME THIS MOUNTAIN!

Friend, no great leader ever received followership or influence on a platter of gold. We've already established that the home turf is the highest sphere of influence for a leader to conquer and command followership. Also, the family is one mountain you would have to conquer on your leadership journey.

You might wonder, "Why is it a mountain?" It is a mountain because if you don't have the right support and influence in your family, it can shorten your leadership adventure. They can become an obstacle.

However, if they are in your corner rooting for you, then you are on your way to resounding success. For instance, Jesus' brothers helped to further the gospel. They helped to make Him a success.

Equally, families run some of the greatest businesses today. One man had the idea and his whole family through his excellent leadership rallied around him to make it grow.

To illustrate, let's take a look at Walmart. It is the largest retailer in the world. The brain behind this business was a man named Sam Walton, who founded the business in 1962. He made it grow and branch out into thousands of stores across the world. Although Sam was such a genius and had great business acumen, he couldn't continue to oversee his empire. He kicked the bucket and passed on in 1992. But His wife and children took over the business and made it more successful.

There are benefits to having support from your family as a leader, business owner, or career person. Therefore, you need to take this mountain. You need to have the same attitude as Caleb. When he was 80 years old, he sought permission from Joshua to go and take over the territory God had promised Him. Don't be satisfied with the influence you already have abroad; you need support back at home.

In so doing, when the rest of the world becomes doubtful of your abilities, skills, and direction, the people have watched you evolve will vouch for you. When you begin to lose grip on the hearts of your followers, your family would say to everyone else, "We have watched him become this person. He's legit."

Again, you cannot ignore the state of your family's heart towards you. Pay attention to what they think of you because they are as crucial to your leadership as the approval of kings and queens in distant kingdoms.

In contrast, one negative word from a person close to home could ruin everything that you have built over the years outside your home circle. Even as you influence people outside of your home, ensure you carry your family along in your growth and progress. Let them know who you are.

Paul wrote to his son, Timothy about those he should appoint as leaders in the church at Ephesus he gave him specifications. He said the leader must be able to provide leadership for his household first. Interesting, right? So part of the duties of leadership is to conquer this mountain and establish your influence in your family. For as Jesus didn't start with His family's approval but earned it, you too will have to earn yours.

JOSEPH EARNED HOME SUPPORT

"And he told it to his father, and to his brethren: and his father rebuked him, and said unto him, what is this dream that thou hast dreamed? Shall I and thy mother and thy brethren indeed come to bow down ourselves to thee to the earth?"

GENESIS 37:10

Joseph the dreamer's story is familiar. At seventeen, God revealed to Joseph through dreams that He had a great plan for him. The young man who fed his father's sheep would dream and see his whole family bowing before him.

In the first instance, he and his family were binding sheaves in the field. Then, his sheaf rose and stood upright, and the sheaves of his family members stood around and paid obeisance to it. In the second dream, Joseph saw the sun, the moon, and the eleven stars paying obeisance to him.

Now, Joseph was the eleventh child, so he had ten elder brothers. Someone in Joseph's position, almost the last child, should not share such a dream. However, he was young. These things both puzzled and excited him, so he told his family.

Well, you can guess what happened. Joseph's father rebuked him for it, and his brothers hated him. They had little faith in him because they only saw him as little Joseph who fed the sheep. His siblings sought to kill him and sold him into slavery. They believed his dream would amount to nothing. But what happened?

Joseph went into Egypt as a slave and became the Prime Minister. The seed of greatness in him grew and branched out. Finally, the world saw him for who he was; an influential leader. However, Joseph only had influence abroad; he didn't have this recognition on home turf. This wasn't enough for God. God's dream for Joseph was for him to have limitless influence.

As time went on, God finally fulfilled what He had revealed to Joseph all those years. The great famine in Canaan brought his brothers to Egypt to find grain. On getting to Egypt, they had to pay obeisance to the Prime minister in charge of the grain. They bowed themselves before him, not knowing they were bowing before their little brother Joseph, thus fulfilling his dream.

Imagine if he had said to himself, "These people who did not believe in me? Let me show them that I'm big now, and they are nowhere close to where I am."

No! Even with his dysfunctional family, he maintained his integrity and showed himself as a true leader. With his actions, he did not need to tell them he was wise and great; they could see his wisdom in the way he treated them. He showed them, and so he did not need to convince them. That truly earned his home support and recognition.

Joseph's case is similar to Jesus's. He had to conquer this family mountain, and the Bible records that His whole family followed him to Egypt. What a great leader! But He didn't start that way. Nevertheless, he earned it by staying true to himself and the vision that God gave him.

JEPHTHAH EARNED HOME SUPPORT

Jephthah was a mighty man of valor but was born out of wedlock. So, when it came time for him to receive a portion of his father's inheritance, his brothers chased him away. They refused to allow him to inherit anything of their father's because he was an illegitimate child.

I want you to consider something for a minute. Didn't we just read he was a mighty man of valor? Yet his family had no use for him. They didn't support or recognize him. They threw him out, and Jephthah ran way.

Although his family rejected him, Jephthah dwelled in the land of Tob, and there he increased in influence. His leadership ability was so great that he went to a strange land and there, commanded followership.

As time went on, the Ammonites laid siege on Israel to destroy it. Consequently, Jephthah's family remembered him. Suffering caused them to realize that they had a mighty warrior in their family doing exploits abroad. Hastily, the elders of Gilead went to Jephthah to seek his help in defeating the Ammonites.

At first, Jephthah refused to help. He was still hurting from their rejection. But the elders of Gilead apologized for their wickedness and promised to make him their head.

Can you see a pattern here, friend? Jephthah's family, like Jesus and Joseph's family, didn't believe in him initially, but they later came to him for help. He earned their support and recognition by delivering them from the Ammonites. He conquered the family mountain and established his influence.

DAVID EARNED HOME SUPPORT

Finally, let's look at David, the son of Jesse and the youngest of eight brothers. Three of his brothers were mighty warriors. They all had the critical job of keeping the country safe while David kept the sheep, which he did with a great sense of duty.

However, David also didn't have recognition and support from his family at first. He had to earn it. David's case was not contempt as it was in Jephthah and Joseph's. They simply ignored him. They expected nothing glorious to come out of him.

You can see the little regard David's family had for him in two instances. The first was when Samuel, the Prophet, came to offer sacrifices at Jesse's house and to anoint the next king of Israel. Samuel asked Jesse to summon all his sons to the sacrifice. David's father obeyed the Prophet; he called out all his sons and paraded them before Samuel. His only error was that he didn't remember David.

I bet he felt David had no place in such an important gathering. He wasn't a warrior like Jesse's other sons. He was only good for keeping sheep and nothing else. But it turned out to be that David was just the person Samuel was looking for.

The second instance was when the Philistines made war against the children of Israel. They paraded their champion, Goliath, before the host of Israel. The giant was a formidable opponent, and he knew it. He challenged the armies of Israel to bring forward their champion to do battle with Him. The Bible records he did this twice a day for forty days. All of Israel were dismayed and much afraid.

While all these things happened, Jesse asked David to take food to his brothers on the battlefield. On getting to the valley where the armies of Israel made war with the Philistines. David saw Goliath come up to make his challenge yet again. When David saw everything that transpired, he got interested.

And he asked what would be done to the man who defeated the giant. Then, family unbelief came to confront him. 1Samuel 17:28 reveals that when his eldest brother, Eliab, heard what David asked, he grew angry and accused David of pride and naughtiness.

Eliab saw David as a naughty little fellow. He never for once thought David was sincerely interested. Since he thought of him only as a child, he felt David came out of child-like curiosity.

But I assure you that David wasn't considered a child for long. As time went on, he proved he was a great leader. He defeated Goliath and led the Israelites to many more victories. And even when David hid from King Saul at the cave of Adullam, his family came to him. 1Samuel 22:1 says, "…when his brethren and all his father's house heard it, they went down thither to him."

Can you see this? The same people who thought little of him are now seeking his leadership. They are now offering their support. David also earned home support and recognition.

We've looked at Joseph, Jephthah, and David, three men who were all leaders in different capacities. They were all ignored and even rejected at first but finally became influential at home. How did they do it? Each man remained true to himself, faithful to God, and pursued his dream.

Sadly, many leaders have failed to command influence and followership among their family members because they have compromised their standards. They didn't remain true to themselves or God and allowed others to sway them from following after their dream or vision.

All these men turned out to be not just good leaders, but great leaders.

NELSON MANDELA NEGLECTED THIS MOUNTAIN

Nelson Mandela was South Africa's first black head of state. He was known for his activities against apartheid in the fight for freedom in South Africa.

In the public eye, Nelson Mandela was a great man. He wielded such great influence and was honored by the world's greatest leaders. In fact, Mandela's assistant, Zelda La Grange, revealed that Nelson Mandela was the only world leader who didn't address Queen Elizabeth of England with the formal "Your majesty" or "Ma'am." He called her Elizabeth. And she held him in high esteem.

But Mandela wasn't a great man at home. He didn't take the time to make an impression or provide passionate leadership. When he and his wife Winnie got married, he was undergoing trial for treason so they couldn't have a honeymoon like an average couple. He was also banned by the South African government and was prohibited from appearing in public gatherings.

Also, Mandela's political career distanced him from his wife. He also didn't involve her in his political life. He kept many secrets and claimed it was for her protection. Mandela spent 27 of their 34 years together in prison.

Winnie never had a chance to know her husband. People always crowded their home. Besides, the security police frequently invaded their privacy or members of Mandela's party, who came to visit unannounced.

Much later, Winnie despised his political career because he was more devoted to it than their marriage. And to spend more time with her husband, she involved herself in politics.

Mandela and Winnie gave birth to two beautiful daughters, but he wasn't around during most of their childhood. In fact, he wasn't around when they were born and was never a family man. He never satisfied the emotional needs of his wife and daughters. For he was ready to sacrifice family life for the freedom of his country. He expected his family to understand his sacrifice.

Mandela didn't conquer the family mountain. He failed to rule his own home. As time went on, all that neglect and absence from home resulted in much crisis.

Although Mandela was a good man who fought for freedom, his wife became a villain. She detained and oppressed youths in her home. On his release from prison, Mandela, out of guilt, had to support his wife facing assault and kidnap charges. Years later, Mandela and Winnie finally separated.

Alas, Mandela's family is dysfunctional, probably because of his inability or unwillingness to conquer this mountain. His children and grandchildren are at each other's necks, fighting over his vast wealth and legacy. The great revolutionary and philanthropists have inspired millions all over the world. He is a peace symbol, but he failed to influence his family.

Moreover, his wasn't a case of being rejected by his family. He didn't give them a chance to accept him. Yes, they believed in him as a great man in the world. But he wasn't a great man in his family.

So, in everything that you do, as you conquer mountains all around the world, remember to go home and build up the same energy there. Because good leaders influence people, but great leaders have limitless influence. They have home support and recognition.

LESSON 3

FRIENDSHIP, OPINION, AND DUTY

A leader is a decision-maker. Moreover, as humans, factors beyond logic and reason always influence our decisions. Relationships and emotions are top on the list of several factors that influence human decisions. Yet, rediscovering the principles of relationships and understanding our humanity will help us adopt a better approach to leadership.

Humanity means receptivity to people's ideas and feelings as to social species. Our relationships have become a trigger for the development of influences that alter the outcome of our leadership metamorphosis.

Consequently, our level of productivity is often subject to the quality of friends we keep, and relationships in our lives. People say, "show me your friend, and I'll tell you who you are." Does this mean, we are a product of people we relate with every day?

Naturally, like the scent we carry after a visit to a smoke-filled room, people's character often rubs off on us. Association and socialization have brought us to a place where we exhibit other people's nature, consciously, or unconsciously.

Studies abound that show responses and reactions in our brains as we relate with others. And most of our thought processes and behaviors have been revealed to come from interacting with people.

A study of participants revealed the relation between happiness to friendship. Ten percent turned out happier than the other ninety because they were part of at least one cherished relationship. What an interesting revelation of the massive influence of relationships in shaping the quality of our personality and wellbeing! Likewise, for instance, family influences our life at home, school revolves around life with teachers and classmates. And work revolves around life with

31

employers, employees, and colleagues. Hence, we have a natural tendency to please and impress people in our lives. How could we survive without relationships?

WHAT ARE FRIENDS FOR?

Leadership can be exhausting, thus making it necessary for people to surround themselves with those they love, accept, and understand. Friendship creates a perfect environment for increased productivity and efficiency. Have you considered democracy– the government of the people, by the people and for the people? DO you realize the *people-centered* politics and leadership style that has been widely accepted? In a democratic government, leaders succeed by drawing closer to feel the needs of their followers. Indeed, leadership or government outside the people, without the people, and against the people cannot stand. Have you considered the place of relationships in your leadership destiny?

HORSES WITHOUT BRIDLE

Horse riding can be majestic and exciting. But, the strength and power of a horse without its bridle will only lead to disaster. The leader's bridle is the counsel and advice that he or she gets from listening to people. A leader's passion, power, and progress can turn dangerous without sensitivity and humanity.

Of course, the greatest leaders in history stood out because they were willing to take advice from people. For instance, Otto Von Bismarck, former German Chancellor, is famous for saying, "a statesman must wait until he hears the steps of God sounding through events, then leaps up and grasp the hem of His garment." Hearing the voice of friends and acquaintances can be as good as the voice of God in certain situations.

For King David, Ahithophel's counsel was like hearing the voice of God. Pharaoh ruled Egypt by Joseph's advice. King Nebuchadnezzar rested heavily on Daniel's wisdom.

Also, consider the Cuban Missile Crisis of the cold war. The cold war was an ideological war between the Eastern communist bloc led by Russia, and the Western capitalist block led America.

In my opinion, the most perilous moment of the cold war was the Cuban Missile Crisis, also known as the Missile Scare. A thirteen-year confrontation ensued between the United States and the Soviet Union because of the unearthing of soviet nuclear facilities in Cuba.

The situation would have escalated into a full-blown nuclear war. However, President John F. Kennedy spent time listening to the opinions of his advisers instead of taking independent or rash decisions before deciding how to handle the situation.

Have you considered Moses? If you know the story of Moses and Jethro, you'll value meekness and relationship. Moses' father-in-law, Jethro, visited him in the wilderness, and he noticed a flaw in Moses' leadership style. He saw that Moses' failure to delegate duties by raising other leaders was taking a toll on him and the newly liberated, but highly undisciplined Hebrews.

So, Jethro advised Moses to seek the path of peace and rest by entrusting many more people to carry the burden of leadership alongside him. Then the Bible said, "**Moses took Jethro's advice** and *chose capable men from among all the Israelites. He appointed them as leaders of thousands, hundreds, fifties, and tens. They served as judges for the people on a permanent basis, bringing the difficult cases to Moses but deciding the smaller disputes themselves"*. Moses chose and trained God-fearing men performed special duties on his behalf.

So, by listening to the advice of his father-in-law Moses improved his effectiveness as a leader. Jethro's advice was like the voice of God, exactly what he needed to hear.

Some leaders have made bad decisions that led to their downfall because of not listening to those around them. Two Biblical examples are Absalom, son of David and Rehoboam, son of King Solomon. Isn't it a wonder that such wise kings had sons who made such foolish decisions?

When Absalom betrayed his father and tried to take his throne, one of David's most trusted advisers – Ahithophel, supported him. As we have seen earlier, his counsel was so valuable that the Bible says that his words were like that of God. However, when Ahithophel gave Absalom advice on how to defeat David, his father, he rejected it. This refusal to listen was a costly mistake. Ahithophel was so confident that he decided to commit suicide, just because Absalom rejected his **super-smart, god-level** advice. However, Absalom also failed and died after he rejected Ahithophel's advice.

What about Rehoboam, who rejected the advice of the elders of Israel? Instead, the naïve king listened to his friends. And this led to having ten out of twelve tribes of Israel pull out from the united confederacy.

THREE WAYS OF RESPONDING TO PEOPLE'S OPINION

Although listening skills are very crucial to effective leadership, yet great leaders understand the power of deciphering other people's opinions. What makes a leader is his ability to filter the advice he gets from people. A great leader should choose the best line of action among different opinions.

Great leaders are not too independent to consider other people's opinion. And they aren't too wise to act based on sound reasoning and not based on emotions, bias, or prejudice.

Some psychologists divide emotions that influence decision-making into two: **anticipated** and **immediate** emotions.

Anticipated emotions are feelings from considering how the other person will feel because of the outcome of our choices, whether positive or negative. And this is not an emotion that is felt when decisions are being made, but before we make decisions.

On the other hand, the decision-making process always produces an experience called: **immediate emotions**. This links reasoning with physically experienced components within the autonomic nervous system and outward emotional expressions.

These emotions that spring up may not even be related to the decision at hand, or they might arise because of environmental influences or temperament. All the same, these emotions have a way of influencing our decision pathway either directly or incidentally.

a. Some leaders reject and suppress other people related to.

You would think this action stems from an abundance of confidence and decisiveness. However, most leaders who do this are insecure and fear rivalry. For instance, George Orwell's novel, titled *Nineteen Eighty-four (1948),* was a clear warning against totalitarianism. Its plot describes this suppressive leadership perfectly.

The book talks about leadership that brainwashes its citizens and suppresses free thought. The populace remained zombies. And any opinion opposite their leader, "Big Brother," was an offense punishable by death. The ruling party is called the "all-controlling party," and the government's policy that enforces the party's doctrine as the only thought was the "thought police."

b. Leaders scared of people's opinions.

Considering the work of George Orwell, although his work was fictional, in 1949, yet he predicted a rise in totalitarian and tyrannical leadership. As a leader, you need not be afraid of people's opinions. Some could be helpful because no one is a bank of knowledge. Everyone should be open to learning and receptive to new ideas.

Embrace criticism, as this will help you know where you are performing well, and where you're not. In as much as being responsible for your actions, it is necessary that you listen to people too. Being fully aware that no one is an island, you must realize we need people to succeed.

c. Some leaders have their own opinions but always prefer or choose other people's opinions over theirs.

This kind of leader is a people-pleaser. Other people's love, approval, and acceptance of what he does are what constitutes real success to him or her. But things like growth, development, and improvement in the standards of living of people should have been the focus. Most times, these kinds of leaders are people with terrible childhood experiences.

They were possibly abused, mocked, underestimated, or bullied, and this made them depend on friends and relatives for defense and support. Do you realize how poor that person's opinion of his abilities would be?

For instance, Jesus' work ethic; He didn't allow personal relationships with people to interfere with His assignment. After John, the beloved, Peter was Jesus' closest disciple. He was more vocal and eager to please his master. As time went by, Peter became more intimate with Jesus and probably believed he had a form of influence on Jesus.

The Bible reveals that when Jesus got closer to His death, He shared His thoughts with His disciples, speaking of all the things He had to pass through. What Peter did was a little bit surprising. The bible records that he took Jesus aside and began to scold Him! Jesus' quick response was to rebuke Peter. The fisherman had forgotten his place and didn't realize that Jesus was now talking about divine work.. Jesus refused to let Peter influence His assignment through his 'kind' close relationship.

There's also the passive response, where a leader has no personal opinions but accepts whatever others say without thinking. Such leaders are spineless and without convictions. People follow those who know what they are doing—those who can stand their ground in the face of crisis and opposition. A leader without an opinion of his/her own is passionless.

Someone who doesn't speak up when things are going wrong is also a perpetrator of that evil, a plus to that crime. An example of such leaders was Eli the Priest. He knew his sons were dishonoring

God and perverting justice, yet he didn't confront them with the truth. Perhaps, he revered and honored them above God.

He was passive to their crimes and atrocities. You would think that being passive excluded him from their wrongs. However, God said to Eli, *"Wherefore kick ye at my sacrifice and at mine offering, which I have commanded in my habitation; and **honourest thy sons above me,** to make yourselves fat with the chiefest of all the offerings of Israel my people?".*

God spoke to him as a culprit. In fact, God addressed Eli as the principal offender, and he received the same punishment as his sons. Eli's bad leadership affected not only his family but also affected the whole nation. A leader must remember that righteousness exalts a nation, but sin is a reproach to all people.

d. Then there is a response whereby the leader can weigh opinions and choose the best one regardless of where it is coming from. He is not too proud or insecure to accept good advice, and he is also not controlled by those around him. A person who responds this way displays a considerable amount of wisdom.

When we talk about wisdom, a man's name often comes to mind. No wonder people say, "as wise as Solomon." King Solomon was one of the wisest kings that ever lived. His first display of kingly wisdom was in the controversy involving two women and a dead child. I'm sure you've read or heard the story before. The story is found in 1 kings 3:16-28.

And just in case you've not heard or read the story, here is a succinct account: two harlots had gone to bed the previous night, both slept with their child by their side. But something unfortunate happened during the night.

One mother had slept on her child and killed it. When the guilty woman noticed this, she quickly switched her baby with that of her mate. Guess what happened in the morning? What mother doesn't recognize her child? The two women dragged each other to the king's court. One was eloquent and very convincing, and able to present her facts prudently.

Have you been before people who are natural orators and able to use words to their advantage? At such moments, wisdom in leadership is highly necessary. Now, the king had to decide who goes home with the child. The other woman was speechless and in pain as the king observed her teary face. She wasn't as convincing as the other woman. In matters of litigation, words are powerful, and content is king. But far more significant than oratory, is the ability to discern.

This discerning king feigned confusion. He proposed that since both women laid claim on the living child, the baby should be cut in two and given to them. While the very composed woman supported the idea, the other soft-spoken woman crying uncontrollably for her child, said something very striking, which paralleled with the thoughts of the king.

She pleaded that the child's life is spared and given to the other woman. Ultimately the liar was exposed, and the king's decision became glaring. A deep cry sprang from the owner of the child and revealed the truth before all observers. The crowd that had gathered in the king's court was amazed—and excited by the ability of the king to calm himself despite their emotional display. He had taken the path of wisdom and discernment and, by so doing, dug out the truth from the chasm of lies, wickedness, and betrayal. If you were in Solomon's shoes, would you have judged based on emotions or pursue the truth with objectivity in search of discernment?

THE MAJORITY ARE NOT ALWAYS RIGHT

Society today is saturated with biased opinions of the majority. Booker T. Washington, an American author and adviser to multiple presidents of the United States, once said, *"A lie doesn't become truth, a wrong doesn't become right, and evil doesn't become good just because the society accepts it."*

The truth is that the majority can be wrong. There is a belief that one man cannot be right and everybody else wrong. You hear supposedly wise sayings about the strength of popular opinion like, "the majority carries the vote," "if you can't beat them join them."

Interestingly, there are instances in history and the bible, where the majority were wrong. Take, for instance, the Wright brothers – Orville and Wilbur, American pioneers of aviation. They rose to limelight for inventing, completing, and flying the world's first real airplane.

But, before their invention became a huge success, they hit a brick wall. Two years after the first successful testing of their invention, the Wright flier went in search of sponsors and potential investors in the project. The plane they built had traveled only 120 feet and lasted only 12 seconds in the air.

But to continue their work, they needed financial support. Unfortunately, most investors didn't believe in their invention. Their dream seems like a white elephant project with no prospects. Their biggest frustration was when the US military turned them down because they believed a flying a plane wasn't realistic.

Alas, they were men standing alone with their dreams and convictions. But, what if they gave in to popular opinion or to the well-meaning encouragements from friends to move on? What do we have today? Different air transport machines as a testament to their achievements and results. Those who have been given the responsibility of achieving great things as leaders, inventors, or even employers must not allow discouragement either from their inner circle, or acquaintances.

From scriptures, do you remember how the Israelites sinned against God in the wilderness? They were tired of waiting for Moses and turned to idol worship. The bible says, "*And when the people saw that Moses delayed to come down out of the mount, the people gathered themselves together unto Aaron, and said unto him, Up, make us gods, which shall go before us; for as for this Moses, the man that brought us up out of the land of Egypt, we wot not what is become of him*".

While Moses delayed, the children of Israel asked Aaron to make them an idol. This was what the crowd wanted, and as a High Priest, Aaron could either stand against their desires or stand-alone to please God. However, Aaron succumbed to the demands of the majority, which was an awful decision to make as a leader.

On the other hand, Jesus was a leader who never followed the crowd in His decisions. The thoughts and ideas He expressed in His teachings were new and revolutionary to the audience. There was an instance in John chapter 6, where He ignored the clamor of the people. Jesus had just supernaturally multiplied food to feed the multitude who were numbered about five thousand men (excluding the women and children).

The people were amazed that they planned to make Him king. But Jesus' convictions and opinions were different from the crowd. Rather than budge, He simply walked away in pursuit of His vision.

Late Dr. Myles Munroe, an ordained minister, author, life coach, and leadership consultant, once said, "you cannot lead the crowd by being part of them. If you want to be a leader, you have to choose a lonely life. You have to turn your back on the crowd. Great leaders are upfront. You can't lead an orchestra without turning your back on the crowd".

Truth is, most leaders cannot make decisions that oppose that of the majority. They anticipate the outcome of bold and unpopular decisions and can't live the consequences. Some fear being disliked or confronted by their followers. They don't want to offend people close to them because they dread loneliness, and such leaders don't end up as great leaders. These are the reason most leaders mix friendship or relationships with work.

A LEADER'S DUTY

Understand that leadership is not for the faint-hearted. Why do you think most leadership coaches use the attitude of a lion rather than a sheep to describe a leader? Do you know that although lions have their pride and their inner circle, yet they often move alone? The bible says that a lion is the strongest among beasts and doesn't turn aside for any other.

So, a leader ought to stay on course without wavering. Jesus had followers, but He carried the cross alone. Leaders are destined to pay the greatest sacrifice, just like Jesus did by dying to save His followers.

As the captain of the ship, you have to be free of emotional influences and prejudice. Moses was a good leader, but he let his followers influence him into making emotional decisions that produced negative results. The Bible says that before a man builds a house, he has to count the cost. In Moses' case, his issue was anger. What about you?

Many people assume vital positions without considering the sacrifices they will need to make. Jesus wholly embraced the cost of leadership. He taught His disciples some of these principles. He told them that if they were to follow His path, they would have to leave their families and all that they hold dear.

Although, He wasn't talking about literally leaving as Abraham did. What He meant was the burden of standing alone in your conviction. Everybody dear to you might disagree with you as a leader, your close companions might misunderstand your vision and even oppose you, but you must persevere.

And because the duty of leadership is critical; leaders have to deal with things that can deter them. Whatever your issue is as a leader, discover it early, so they don't later work against you. However, we have our shortcomings that are sometimes inevitable. It should not be heard of God's leaders that they wallowed in their weaknesses, rather than seeking for divine strength. People will always be around to give suggestions, but you alone can decide. You must be able to rise above people's influence and control in your decision-making.

HOW TO RISE ABOVE PEOPLE'S OPINIONS

To rise above general opinions, you should be able to manage your emotions. Emotional intelligence is very crucial in achieving success in leadership. Have you ever felt like your friend would get hurt, or feel bad if you didn't buy their idea? We all want to have a beautiful relationship with both our friends and family members, but they should not be the drivers of our vision. It's ok if they advise, but you must decide which one to stick to. There are also certain attributes expected of a leader. God expects that we exhibit Godly attributes as leaders and not otherwise. Here are some qualities of a great leader:

1. A leader must exercise great patience: Someone said, "Success doesn't teach us how to be successful, failure does. Most leaders are easily influenced by others for fear of failure. Are you scared your idea might fail? Or people might not support you? You should be patient with that vision, that idea, and see it to the end.

   Successful people were once great failures who decided to keep on failing. They didn't hang their boots when they failed! They camped on that idea, conviction, or invention like a hen hatching eggs until they produced results.

   Don't rush into things because of the heat of the moment, and don't rush out either. Take, for instance, Thomas Edison's teachers wrote him off as a retard. They said he was too stupid to learn anything. While inventing the light bulb, he tried one thousand times and was unsuccessful. Can you imagine that? I believe his friends and family must have told him to move on. But he was patient with the idea. He could see the future.

   Most leaders make impatient and rash in their decisions because they don't see into the future. Later, when a reporter asked Edison how he handled his numerous failures, his reply was shocking and delightful! He told the reporter that he did not fail a thousand times but that his invention had one thousand steps! Earlier I spoke of President John F. Kennedy's ability to properly handle the Cuban Missile Crisis.

   The truth is, only great leaders can exercise such a level of patience. People who act emotionally always end up in regrets. Do you want to be a great leader? Learn to be patient with your ideas.

2. A leader must be calm: Do you know that calmness is a psychological state? It is very effective in dealing with negative emotions like anxiety, stress, anger, and frustration. It is believed that calmness deepens our ability to connect with people and sharpens our focus. Breathe deeply often, especially before meetings or gatherings that could cause you to feel stressed or anxious. Maintain positive thoughts – Avoid thinking about

people's negative opinions of you or your close friend's view about your actions. Don't lose your peace. Be calm. Understand that most people are emotional in their response. So, avoid being pressurized

3. Cut off unholy ties: Take, for instance, David and Joab. Joab was the captain of David's army. He was also his aid and supporter in perpetrating evil acts. Do you remember how the king slept with a married woman and killed her husband? Lack of integrity in leaders give people a foothold.

    Joab also defied David often because he had lost credibility and respect in his eyes. He killed Abner who came to reconcile with David. This displeased David so much that he laid a curse on Joab and his household. Joab later killed Absalom, King David's son, despite David's instructions not to harm the young man.

    You see, perpetuating evil before your followers will make them override your instruction. When you lack character, you lose influence also.

4. Build intellectual capacity: Lack of adequate knowledge can cause a leader to be easily controlled by other people's opinions. Not knowing what to do at any point depicts incompetence and ignorance. Therefore, ask God for wisdom.

    When you demonstrate great wisdom people, value your opinion. Consider Solomon, who asked God for wisdom and see how it played out in his life. Learning must become natural for a leader because your knowledge will be tested. You inspire influence through your knowledge.

    Therefore, read books. Learn from Jesus. He was a leader who always wanted to be informed about public opinion yet was complete in Himself. He didn't need people's opinions to be confident. He had inner authority, and this made Him an influential leader because He stood alone in His convictions. Although He was killed, the fruits of such dynamic and powerful leadership speak for itself today in the rapid growth and influence of Christianity.

Finally

Leadership is very vital, and it comes with diverse responsibilities. A leader is a person of mighty valor and strength. If you must be a successful leader, you need to watch your circle of friends and the external factors, which influence your actions. It's very expedient to have friends as a leader and to seek for advice, where your strength can't carry.

But there has to be a clear-cut definition of duty and relationship. Leaders have followers, and to keep them, they must know what to do at every point. Let there be a healthy boundary between "leadership and friendship," so our emotions doesn't overwhelm us when we need to make critical decisions.

Do you feel like your friends are in total control of your leadership? Do you think of yourself as not accomplishing what God demands from you as a leader? This is the right time for you to turn back to God, who called you into leadership. God is your ultimate help, and He alone can give you the wisdom needed to carry out the duties expected to lead rightly.

If you go to God for wisdom, He will give it to you, without finding fault. The Bible says in James 1:5, *"If any of you lacks wisdom, let him ask God, who gives generously to all without reproach, and it will be given him."* You can have this benefit by first having a relationship with God, and it starts by acknowledging that you are a sinner, then accepting Christ as your personal Lord and Saviour. *"Seek ye first the kingdom of God, and all these things shall be added unto you."* A popular saying goes thus "first thing first." We must do the needful to be beneficiaries of what accompanies it.

There is a way you carry yourself as a leader, which will determine how people relate to you. There must be lines that cannot be crossed, you must be a great leader and also maintain your relationship with friends and acquaintances. This balance is what makes you a great leader.

LESSON 4

OPTIMISM AND COURAGE

Optimism is the foundation of courage

Nicholas M. Butler

I once saw a quote that reads, "I will love the light for it shows me the way, yet I will endure the darkness because it shows me the stars." What an incredible perspective! You see, extraordinary leadership is about having a brighter perspective. Great leaders see opportunity and victory, where others see obstacles and defeat. They are willing to go where others are afraid to go and do what others are scared to do.

So, I think it's only natural to trustingly follow a man who can see beauty in chaos, an advantage in a setback. The man who can see (like the bible says) "a lifting up when there is a casting down."

The world is already on top speed to become an impossible place to live in. The man who will be a great leader is the one who can create the possibilities others only dream of. Success and greatness only exist because there are failures and mediocrity. The former happens when the latter has been challenged and conquered. The same way, victory would be needless without battles.

It was Eleanor Roosevelt who made this remarkable statement: "You gain strength, courage, and confidence by every experience in which you really stop to look fear in the face. You are able to say to yourself, 'I lived through this horror. I can take the next thing that comes along.'"

Think about it for a moment!

Captains of the ship to glory and power are men and women of great optimism and courage. No one can pursue a vision without being

45

positive about the future. And, neither can champions emerge without confronting challengers.

Jesus was a leader who had these qualities in spades. But He didn't just manifest optimism and courage. He taught it too. He inspired His disciples to have a positive outlook and a strong heart. His sermon on the mount can be seen as a military drill. He knew the world was going to be a tough place for them to live in without Him around, so He taught them the attitudes that would guarantee their success. Personally, I think the most optimistic and courage inspiring verses in Matthew chapter are 5 are verses 10 and 11. It says, "Blessed are they which are persecuted for righteousness' sake: for theirs is the kingdom of Heaven. Blessed are ye, when men shall revile you, and persecute you, and shall say all manner of evil against you falsely, for my sake".

HEARTTITUDE

"And it was so that when he(Saul) had turned his back to go from Samuel, God gave him another heart…"

1 SAMUEL 10:9

The first gift God gave King Saul in the bible wasn't a shiny crown or a chariot. No, my friend, God, gave Saul a new heart. The old heart didn't have the capacity for fighting wars, defending territories, and ruling a nation. This goes to prove that leadership is not just an act but much more; it's an attitude. So, what's an attitude? Well, it simply refers to your disposition or behavior because of the way you think. Your attitude is the steering and steam that direct and move your life.

According to the Bible, out of your heart, attitude, or "heartitude" flows the issues of life. Leaders don't lead from their heads, but from their hearts. They lead from their store of beliefs and opinions. Have you ever seen a firefighter in action? He is willing to dash into a burning building to rescue a mother and her a baby while other people watch, cry, or even cheer.

What's the difference between the fireman and the other bystanders? Their heart! This man has had drummed into his heart, an orientation that controls his behavior. So, when he sees a fire, he's not thinking about saving himself, he's considering others. The same goes for leadership.

Some people have cultivated the habit of quitting and surrendering. They see themselves as prey. While others have developed the habit of persevering and challenging their fears. They see themselves as the leader. The only difference between these two groups is the attitude of their heart.

The Bible in proverbs 30:30 says that "the lion is strongest among beasts and doesn't turn away for any." This means that the lion never backs down from a challenge. Have you noticed that the lion doesn't look like the strongest? There are other larger, fiercer looking animals. But the lion's heart is the strongest.

Do you know that the lion sees every other animal as prey, yet isn't prey to any? The thought has never crossed its mind that it can ever be food. However, other beats have designated themselves as food, no wonder they run when they see the lion coming. But the lion will never run. He will only prove to you who the boss is..

Have you seen yourself as food before now? Do you think you're inferior to other people? If yes, then you have to change what you think about yourself because it will affect your teammates or followers negatively.

Many leaders in the bible stood through hard times because they were optimistic and courageous. The attitude of their hearts was one of never-give-up. You might know them; they are Joshua and Caleb.

The book of Numbers chapter 13 tells the story of the twelve spies Moses sent into the land of Canaan. Twelve men went into the same country and saw the same things, but had different opinions and perspectives because of the attitude of their hearts. Ten of the spies that were sent out came back with a negative report.

They said to Moses, "we are not able to go up against the people; for they are stronger than we. The land through which we have gone to search it, is a land that eats up the inhabitants thereof; and all the people that we saw are men of great stature. We were in our own sights like grasshoppers, so we were in their sight."

However, two of the spies who were sent out, Joshua and Caleb, had a different report. They tried to calm the already agitated Israelites down. They said that the land was exceedingly good and that they were able to overcome it.

Consider that these twelve spies were sent to the same place. So why were their reports controversial? Their hearts. The positive two believed they were strong enough to conquer the land, while the negative ten believed they were grasshoppers. The most interesting thing about this story is that the ten spies with the bad report said they were in their own eyes like grasshoppers. So their major problem was the attitude of their hearts, which made them to see obstacles and defeat where others so opportunity and victory.

Years later, when Caleb discussed this event with Joshua, he said he gave a report of the land as it was in his heart. His positive attitude came from deep within him, and he led the children of Israel to victory with his heart.

Your heart's attitude, the way you think or see things, determines the greatness of your leadership. It was Richard Bach, who said, "sooner or later, those who win are those who think they can."

Friend, what's the content of your heart? Do you have a positive or negative attitude? If you were in Caleb's day and age, would you be among the ten spies? Or maybe you've discovered that like Saul, you need a change of heart? Also, the state of your heart controls your perspective. The ten spies saw themselves as grasshoppers.

Furthermore, a leader's attitude is essential when it comes to caring for those he/she is leading, and our Lord Jesus Christ is the perfect example. Jesus had a heart of compassion towards those He met.

I bet you're very familiar with the story of the five loaves and two fishes. But what you might not have noticed is that Jesus's disciples didn't see anything wrong in sending the multitude away without feeding them. Yet Jesus was thinking about their physical as well as spiritual well-being. His natural attitude towards everyone around him was genuine love and care.

He insisted on feeding the people who had spent three days in the wilderness with Him. his logic was that if He sent them away, they would faint on the way. Is it not surprising that in the Bible, whenever a leader with a heart of gold steps up, a miracle is born? If Jesus wasn't the kind of leader, He was there wouldn't have been the miracle of the feeding of the five thousand.

Our hearttitude as leaders matter, not only for confronting challenges and conquering territories but also for caring for those under our watch. The same compassion that moved Jesus to drive out demons from people caused Him to provide emotional support and care.

Do you want to be like a great leader like Jesus? Then you have to adjust your hearttitude today.

WHAT DO YOU SEE?

We are all in the gutters but some of us are looking at the stars

Oscar Wilde

In leadership, people follow the man with the vision, the one who sees things differently. No one can be a great leader without optimism and courage, yet these qualities depend on what you see. Some people see obstacles and dead-ends at every turn. The difference between consumers and inventors is that the latter see opportunity where the former see obstacles.

The stories of great men like the Wright brothers, Thomas Edison, and the like are the tales of people who saw what other people couldn't see. They kept their eyes focused on their vision until they made others see it.

There's a famous saying that if life gives you lemons, make lemonade. This simply means that in every circumstance, you've got to look on the bright side. Successful people focus more on the pros than cons. And successful leaders aren't just people who can see the beauty in chaos but can make others see it too.

Your perspective in life determines your actions. Are you the type that sees the glass as half empty or half full? Do you see a mountain as an obstacle or an elevated platform? Warriors see battles as a chance for peace, while champions see challenges as a sign for victory.

Great leaders can see what isn't there or glaring to everybody. They don't see the world the way it is in all its harshness. They see it as it can be. World changers and great leaders dream for others. What you see will either inspire or discourage you.

This is why optimism and courage are so important. You must develop the ability to always see a way out. To be a great leader, you have to cultivate the habit of seeing opportunities and victories where others see obstacles and defeat.

Jesus always maximized such opportunities to help people. If you read the Acts of the Apostles, you would notice that Peter picked up the same habit. An example of Jesus's ability to maximize opportunities is his encounter with the Samaritan woman at the well. This scene is found in John, chapter 4. Jesus was really thirsty, but he used His need for water to meet the need of the Samaritan woman.

She was in dire need of a savior. She had messed up her life, and she was in the process of doing more damage. While Jesus was at the well, he was able to convince her that He was the Messiah and get her to repent from her sinful lifestyle. Not only did the woman experience salvation that day, but her whole town also. For she went abroad spreading the news of what Jesus had told her and had done to her.

Another example of a leader who was optimistic and courageous was David. He saw what no one else saw. Therefore, he achieved what no one else could achieve.

The Bible tells of the story of David and Goliath in 1Samuel chapter 17. The Philistines made war against the Israelites. Both nations camped on mountains that faced each other and had a valley between them. Out of the camp of the Philistines went a champion whose name was Goliath. He was a giant of a man and a skilled warrior. His height was six cubits and a span.

Goliath challenged the armies of Israel to produce a man that would fight with him. If he (Goliath) was defeated, the philistines were to serve the Israelites, but if otherwise, the Israelites were to serve them. He did this for forty days and forty nights, and the host of Israel, including the King, was afraid. Nobody could see a way around this enormous problem. But along came David.

Three of David's brothers were in the Israeli army and on the battlefield. As a result, David was sent by his father, Jesse to deliver some food to his brothers. Coincidentally, when David got to the battle was the same time, Goliath came out to declare his challenge once again.

When David heard the philistine speak and the reward that awaited whoever defeated him, he got interested and began to ask questions. Meanwhile, word got to King Saul that a certain young man was interested in fighting the giant, so the King sent for him. When David came before Saul, he expressed his idea to take the challenge and fight the giant.

Saul didn't believe in the young fellow, but granted David's request because of his insistence and stories of how God had enabled him to kill a bear and a lion. Once David was endorsed by the King, he drew close to the philistine.

Every man in the camp of the Israelites saw Goliath as a mighty warrior. What they didn't know was that their perspective was what incapacitated them. However, David came with a fresh perspective. He saw Goliath for what he really was.

Now, the Jews are people who have a covenant with God, the sign of which is circumcision. It was based on their covenant with God that became a mighty and prosperous nation. Everything they did was tied to that covenant. Including their victories in warfare.

As a result, when David discussed Goliath with the King, he described him as an uncircumcised philistine. David saw what no one else could see. In David's perspective. Goliath was an easy target because he had no covenant of protection and victory with God.

So he was vulnerable and easy to defeat compared with David, who knew he had God backing him because of the covenant. Secondly, David didn't see the battle as his. He said, "the battle is the Lord's," and the Lord can't lose a battle against a mortal man.

Only the remarkable David saw things in this light. Thirdly, David saw another opportunity to testify of God's help. He told Saul that the philistine would be just like the bear and lion he killed. He would become the content of his testimony.

Lastly, David saw a reward. Beforehand; he repeatedly asked the soldiers around what would be done to the man who defeated Goliath. Do you notice that not once did David consider defeat? This was a young man that the bible described as having the features of a girl. He was so handsome and tender, yet his eyes saw differently.

As a leader, what do you see? Do you see an opportunity for greatness at every turn? Or do you see dead ends? What do you think would have happened if someone like David wasn't at the camp that day? Goliath would have continued prancing around in false glory. Most of the challenges we face are victories in disguise. All we need is the heart to unravel them.

Jesus was a leader who knew greatness when he saw it, even when it looked like a short tax collector. And he saw good where everyone else saw evil. I believe Jesus was such a successful leader because he could see what nobody else saw. Leadership is all about people, and Jesus could see the light in the darkest situations.

If you're looking for an excellent example of optimism, Jesus is the perfect fit. One day while Jesus was walking through a particular city, a ruler of the synagogue named Jairus beckoned on Him. His daughter was very sick and at the point of death. Jesus immediately agreed to follow the worried Father to his home to pray for the little girl. While they were on their way, a small company of people came from the ruler's house bearing bad news. They asked the man not to bother Jesus any further because his daughter dead.

To these people, the case was closed. Nothing could be done. But Jesus was optimistic even in the face of death. He asked the father of the child not to fret. He told him that his daughter wasn't dead but was asleep. Of course, everyone around laughed at Jesus. They were unable to what Jesus saw. Jesus didn't see death but an opportunity for God to be glorified.

On getting to Jairus' house, Jesus put everyone out of the room. I believe He didn't want their negative energy interfering with God's plans. When He was finally alone with the little girl, he simply called out to her, and she woke up. Jesus knew what God could do. He looked beyond the obstacle, which was death. Jesus never saw defeat, only victory. What do you see?

BE STRONG AND COURAGEOUS

Success is not final; failure is not fatal: but is the courage to continue that counts.

Winston S. Churchill

When God commissioned Joshua to replace Moses as leader of Israel, He repeated the same phrase three times. The phrase was "be strong and courageous." God, through these words, was telling Joshua that leadership had battles that would require his strength and challenges that would demand his courage. God wasn't mincing words. He didn't give Joshua a perfect picture of Leadership. Weakness and fear were going to be threats to his success, but he had to overcome them.

There's a famous saying that courage is not the absence of fear, but it is forging ahead despite it. Sprinters will tell you that their victory lap is when they feel out of breath the most. The battle is at its hottest before the victory. It is this way so that only those truly dedicated to victory can become champions.

Every great leader must learn how to forge ahead amid tremendous difficulty. Come to think of it, leadership exists because someone has to do the job that everyone else can't. Joshua was going to face some significant challenges, but what would determine his greatness won't be his ability to avoid challenges but confront them.

All great leaders are confronters. Remember David, who confronted Goliath? What about Moses, who kept leading the Israelites towards the Red Sea. At first, the Red Sea was an obstacle, but because a leader was strong and courageous, it became a highway to walk through.

The truth is, when it comes to leadership, real success can't be attained without sailing through foggy waters and rough seas. There'll be times when nobody believes in you but yourself. David had such an experience at Ziklag, when his men thought of stoning because they grieved for their wives and kids.

He had also lost his wives and kids too. But while his men were looking for who to blame, he was trying to muster the courage. He knew he had to think differently because he was the leader. The bible says that David encouraged himself in God and got God's word to pursue, overtake, and recover all.

Most times, when people talk about courage, our minds go to grand larger than life risks our heroes take for the greater good. But what about those everyday actions that reveal strength and courage.

An example of an everyday person who exhibited great courage is an African American woman, named Rosa Parks. She was born on the 4th of February, 1913, in Alabama. Mrs. Parks lived in America in a period where racial segregation was at its harshest.

During this period in the U.S. blacks and whites didn't mix. There were the segregation laws that covered sitting arrangements on the buses. These laws differed according to the area. In Montgomery, the front seats on buses were reserved for white passengers only. And if no white passengers boarded the buses, those seats were to be left vacant.

Also, if the whites occupied all the seats reserved for them, black passengers were expected to vacate their seats for them. The most outrageous part of all this was that the blacks still got to pay the same bus fare as the whites. This was the nature of existence for the blacks at that time.

Moreover, blacks who defied these laws were to be arrested and fined. The drivers were also mandated to remove such an offender from the bus. This was the atmosphere in which the blacks lived during this period. So how does Rosa Parks come in?

In 1955 Mrs. Parks boarded a bus and sat right next to the section reserved for white passengers. She was asked to give up her seat for a white passenger, but she refused. The little black woman had to be forcibly evicted and arrested.

Her action was seen as an act of bravery in all the black communities, and it sparked a nation-wide protest. A year later, blacks combined forces and staged a one-year boycott of the bus services in the United States. This resulted in the review and removal of the bus segregation law.

What this lady did seemed so insignificant. She didn't know the ripple effect of her actions. Courage is contagious. Bravery in a leader will strengthen the weakest follower to achieve great things.

In talking about leaders whose courage in critical situations strengthened others, I'm reminded of Jesus. He's our most exceptional leader of all time and our ultimate example. Now, remember that while Jesus was on earth, he lived as a man and lead as a man. So his leadership style can be easily emulated by anyone who wants to become a great leader.

Mark 4:35-41 brings us on the scene of an exciting story. Jesus and his disciples were retiring for the day. Their afternoon had been hectic, walking around with a multitude hounding your every step can drain the life out of you. When it was evening, Jesus requested that they go over to the other side of the river by boat.

While Jesus and his disciples boarded their ship, other ships joined them, and they were on their way. However, their journey wasn't peaceful for long. A storm came out of nowhere and hit the ships hard. In fact, the vessel carrying Jesus suffered the most damage. The waves beat against the ship so hard that it became full of water.

The disciples were hysterical, they felt they were all going to die. I bet they wondered at this point, "Where in the world is Jesus?" Little did they know that Jesus was sleeping peacefully in the stern on a leather cushion. When they found him, they were heartbroken. They woke him hurriedly, asking if he didn't care that they were all about to drown.

Guess what Jesus did? He just rebuked the wind like it was a piece of cake, and the storm obeyed Him. Jesus didn't panic. Neither did he show a sign that indicated fear of death even for a minute. After the wind had died down, he asked them, "Why are you so fearful? How is it that ye have no faith?"

I bet you'll try and explain Jesus's courage that He was that calm because He was God-man. But that is not what His question to His disciples implies. He expected them to have acted the same way He did. He was showing them how an ideal leader was supposed to be. Totally courageous and entirely in charge. Jesus was a great leader who taught courage and lived it in His everyday life.

DARE TO FAIL

Only those who dare to fail greatly can ever achieve greatly

Robert F. Kennedy

A great man once said that nobody really learns from success; people always learn from failure. However, I believe we get inspired by success despite failure. It seems that failure makes success worthwhile and authentic. So those who have resolved to be successful must also embrace all the failures that help them create their success.

History and the bible revealed to us that the greatest leaders of all times are those who dared to fail. They didn't see failure as too fatal or a barrier, they saw success as too attractive to ignore. We are asked to follow Jesus' example, who for the joy set before him endured the cross, despising the shame. But many of us find that hard to do.

What made Jesus successful was that amid shame and pain, He was able to see joy ahead into His destination. We've repeatedly established how great a leader Jesus was. Indeed, a great leader can see opportunities and victory, where others see obstacles and defeat.

A biblical example of a leader who dared to fail is Queen Esther. The Queen received news from her uncle that her people—the Jews, were being plotted against. A certain influential royal official planned to wipe out all the Jews. But Queen Esther and her Uncle—Mordecai would not stand and watch their people being slaughtered.

The Queen had to pay a very high price. She had to go into the King's inner court to plead her people's course. According to the tradition of the Medes and Persians, it wasn't lawful for anyone to enter into the King's inner court without being summoned.

The punishment for this was death. And, Esther had not been called by the King. Yet, for her people, she considered her life a small sacrifice to pay for the deliverance of her people. This was the circumstance that prompted her to make her famous "if I perish I perish" statement.

The Queen dared failure and gazed fearlessly at death. The result of her action brought resounding success. But some people are unable to look past the risk of failure. Therefore missing out on the crown victory that rightly should be placed on their head. Seeing beyond risks always places you at an advantage in the outcome of your decisions.

Another biblical leader who had what it takes to dare failure was Jesus. Most people fail to read in-between the lines when studying about Jesus. Remember, we've established that the possibility of success also comes with a degree of impossibility and failure. Well, this means that Jesus had every chance of failing. His temptation in the wilderness is a clear indication that He was like any other man. I mean, He could have fallen to Satan's deception. What about when at the garden of Gethsemane where he poured out His heart to God? There He prayed like any other man would have.

His humanity easily reflected in His prayers. He asked God to take away His life's assignment. Why? He saw the weight of the responsibility, and He thought it will be better to do it any other way. The way of the cross was a risky path! But thank God, He yielded to God's will.

Also, think about the many times Jesus went into hiding because He was hunted by wicked men. Jesus was on the most important mission on earth. So, He risked his life at every turn. One thing kept Him moving on—He looked past all the challenges and shame. And kept His gaze on the joy set before Him.

Have you ever thought of how it felt for God to become a baby? Grow up in a neighborhood with other kids? Be spanked by the babysitter? This is on a funnier note. Jesus risked everything by becoming our propitiation for sin. He didn't consider failure even for a minute, and in so doing, he dared to fail.

Friend, do you have the guts to dare failure? Do you see risk as a necessary burden of leadership and success as too attractive to ignore? You might ask, "What if I fail?" failure has never killed anyone. All the successful people we looked at earlier attained success because of what they learned from their failures. Attaining success as a leader is impossible without a resilient heart towards life.

CONCLUSION

Friend, without a doubt, optimism and courage are two companions you don't want to leave behind on your journey to greatness. They will supply you needed strength more than water in the desert, and will ignite your passion and drive than fuel will do in a car.

Jesus always looked on the bright side as a leader. He always saw the best in people and never wrote anybody off. In his relationship with His disciples, you can see His optimism shining through. Even when He was disappointed with their frequent display of faithlessness, he gently scolded them with the hope of them getting better.

I believe Jesus's most significant show of optimism can be seen in His relationship with Peter. Can you imagine that Jesus knew that Peter would betray Him, yet He still worked with Him? What would you have done if you were in Jesus's place? Would you have been able to trust such a fellow? But Jesus never saw things the way we do.

John 21:15 brings us to a scene after His resurrection. You see Jesus dining with His disciples, who all went into hiding after He was seized by the soldiers and killed. In fact, His absconded disciple— Peter was there. Jesus didn't mention, Peter's error even once. Instead, He spoke about the future. At least, don't you think Jesus could have used Peter to deliver a hot message? Jesus never did that. He left the past and focused on the future!

Also, when it comes to courage, Jesus is our most excellent leadership example. Can you imagine how much courage it took for Jesus to face the pain and shame of the cross? How did He know His sacrifice was going to be accepted or appreciated? His death was a risk, and it took all the courage in the world to lay down His life for us.

You can't be a great leader without optimism and courage. And the fastest way to learn this virtue is to simply lean on Christ and learn of Him.

LESSON 5

SPEAKING WITH CHARACTER AND HONESTY

"Real leadership is being the person others will gladly and confidently follow."

-John C. Maxwell

Imagine for a moment that you have hundreds of eyes watching you as you do your business. They are skillful personnel with bird's eye view, who stealthily take note of what you do when you're away from the public eye. Without fail, they notice how you relate with your spouse, kids, and everyone around you. They have the power to see through your thoughts and know when you tell a lie. Can you imagine if, on a particular day, they decide to come clean and, maybe, reveal all they have observed in a movie—your life's movie?

Someone once said, "Real leaders do not have a private life." Leaders are leaders at all times. Here, on a couple of pages in this chapter, is another life-changing lesson on leadership!

As I progress, I want you to observe this exciting office scenario. You are ready for this. Aren't you?

The Boss: "Ladies and gentlemen, when we hit the "BIG" target for the month, this company will reward everyone with a "fat" bonus!" And, after a few scattered claps, the Boss yells: "So, let's get to work!"

Fast forward to the end of the month, and surprisingly, for the first time in 13 months, employees meet the "BIG" target. Thanks to two newly employed foreign nationals who did the extra work, while the remaining five were secretly slacking. The young men had to work themselves to the bone to impress the Boss. But did they drive that home? Was the Boss really impressed?

60

On the first day in the new month, the Boss walked into the staff meeting, thrilled at the results, and a little surprised! But just as always, like a recorder playing, he gave several shallow remarks and impersonal comments.

"Ladies and gentlemen, Let's do it again!" That was all he said and dismissed the meeting.

Twenty minutes after the meeting, you could still hear hysterical laughter from the old staff. But a different reaction ensued from the new boys. The two new employees gasped in bitter bewilderment and utter dismay. They asked each other and other members a series of depressing questions to which they had no answer.

"What?! Where is the 'FAT' bonus he promised?"

"This is unfair! After our desperate hard work to pull this through? How about some acknowledgment of our input, any recognition?"

"What's going on here? Who is this man? A Leader or a Liar?"

The situation of these employees is a sad story and you may be shaking your head as you read, but this chapter is not about the fictional Boss. This chapter is about you.

WHO ARE YOU?

My friend, words are powerful! How do you treat yours? Words provide direction or create obstacles; they set-in-motion or halt crucial processes; they breathe life or cause death.

This is why John C. Maxwell said, real leaders are people we can gladly and confidently follow. Are you one? How many people can rest on what you say, knowing that you will stand by it? Do you have the character and honesty required to be a LEADER, a man or woman of your words?

Leadership is not by size. As a man's word is, so is his honor; however tall, however short. You can never be more honorable than the quality and integrity of your utterances. Every leader must learn to respect what comes out of their mouth. This is because what their words are the life-source of their influence and the life-blood of their authority.

But saying one thing and acting differently is a serious indicator of an inherent character flaw. Great leaders dare to say **YES** when they need to, and **NO** when the situation demands it –without making promises, they can't keep.

Consider this incredible statement from one of the world's leading coach and author, John C. Maxwell, "People buy into the leader before they buy into the vision." Wow! So, why's it that leaders struggle to make followers own the vision of their team? Why is there so much apathy in corporate settings? Could it be traced to failed promises and empty words?

When you're known for breaking promises, you'll eventually lose influence. I'm sure you already know that leadership is all about influence. But who will trust someone who changes like a chameleon; and say things he can't do, making promises he does not intend to keep? Get this! **People must believe you to follow you.**

You can't argue with the truth, my friend! Know, leadership is for the brave. It's for the man who can afford to stand alone with his vision. And not for the chicken-hearted. The lion is the best animal for describing the strength of a true leader's heart. No wonder the word **"lion-heart."**

Thus, "A lion, mighty among beasts, **RETREATS before nothing.**"[1] The word "retreat" means: "an act of moving back or withdrawing." So, can I ask, when was the last time you backed-off, receded, chickened out, or withdrew from a course you had earlier committed to by the words of your mouth? What does it take to speak with character?

More often than not, leaders fail because they lack courage. They let other people influence them. They compromise, make bad decisions, or make promises they can't keep. It takes courage and strength of

---

[1]Proverbs 30:30 (NIV BIBLE)

heart to stay true to yourself, despite the pressure. No retreat, no surrender.

Therefore, the man who is a great leader is the man that dares to say **YES** when he could recoil and **NO** when the situation demands it. He does not fear to say yes to what is right, yet, he does not make promises he can't keep. Such a person's virtue is vital in leadership. And we'll be calling this virtue or quality; the ability to speak with character and honesty.

WHY PEOPLE MAKE PROMISES THEY CAN'T KEEP

"For every promise, there is a price to pay…"

-Jim Rohn

We've all been caught with our hands in the cookie jar. Can you sincerely say you haven't broken a promise? Well, neither can I. But we can't ignore the importance of keeping our promises, because broken promises equal broken trust. And trust earns you influence as a leader, a husband, a father, a friend. Just name it!

Making a promise is one of the most common forms of expression. We can hardly interact appropriately with others without making them. When we make a promise, we declare our intent to carry out a plan or come through on an agreement. It involves the most important and trivial matters of everyday life. Marriage vows, keeping an appointment, doing your jobs, buying a gift, etc.

Psychologists have done some excellent research that explains why people make promises they can't keep. These facts can help us deal with our issues and become better leaders;

1. To avoid criticism

Here, a person tries to impress others even if he doesn't have the will or capability to fulfill the promise. This person doesn't want to assume a bad name. And can't stand being criticized. However, he or she loses trust eventually.

2. Being afraid to say "NO."

People in this category have insecurity issues. They don't want to be disliked or rejected. As a leader, you must make objective decisions that might not get popular support. But if you're afraid to say no, you'll end compromising your standards.

When a leader has low self-esteem and a morbid craving for acceptance, he strives to please everybody. He would make promises in order to "belong," even if he does not stand the chance of performing it. Doing this will eventually sabotage this vision. A great leader sets clear boundaries. Let people know what you stand for, and be brave enough to watch them leave.

3. Self-delusion or deceit

Don't FAITH a promise. Be sure you can do it. This category refers to people who mean what they say. When they make a promise, they have every intention to carry out. But they don't admit and accept their limitations.

It's okay not to can do something. There's no need saying yes when your resources say no. People who delude themselves cannot predict their capabilities. So they disappoint their teammates, family, etc.

4. Having an ulterior motive

Do you know people make promises they can't keep on purpose? The persons in the previous discussion points are sincere. But the folks in this category are plain mean. They make promises to get people to do what they want.

A perfect example is politicians. They promise their supporters the whole world while running for office. However, after their victory in the polls, they deny ever making such promises. Also, this breach of trust plays out in the workplace and family. A boss gives incentives and doesn't make good on them. A parent promises to give a child a treat if they do well at school but fails to do so.

Usually, in any of the cases, the result is still disastrous.

5. Being emotional

Last, people make promises they can't keep because they let emotions control them. They get excited or happy, so they make a vow on the spur of the moment. Meanwhile, they can choose to act differently. Just as the bible says, "Do not be quick with your mouth, do not be hasty with your heart..."[2]

Circumstances, feelings, and capacities do change. These things aren't constant, so you can't rely on them. I bet you've seen couples who swore to be together forever get divorced. Also, people who promised to help others financially can lose their job; a loved one can die, a child might be born. These are examples of changes in circumstances, feelings, and capacities. Don't allow anything other than sound reasoning to be the basis of your promises. Never leave off your brain when you make a promise.

Friend, can you relate to this? Do you find yourself in these categories? Have you broken trust, and you feel awful? Do you want to make amends? You can do something about it. Again, hear out John C. Maxwell;

"As a leader, you're out in front, casting vision and giving direction. You're vocal and highly visible; your words and deeds affect a lot of people. Eventually, you're going to say or do something that violates another person's trust in you. You'll deliver criticism at the wrong time, speak more harshly than a situation merits, forget to fulfill a promise, etc. However, it's not an initial misstep, but the poor response to it, that does the most damage in a relationship."

Learning to speak with **character** and **honesty** is the remedy of broken promises. These two qualities will undoubtedly provide the strength with which to say **YES** when you need to, and **NO** when the situation demands it.

---

[2]Ecclesiastes 5:2 (NIV BIBLE)

CHARACTER IS KEY

I care not what others think of what I do, but I care much about what I think of what I do! That is character!

Theodore Roosevelt

Jim Rohn, American entrepreneur, author and motivational speaker, said that "Character isn't something you were born with and can't change, like your fingerprints. It's something you weren't born with and must take responsibility for forming."

The Merriam Webster dictionary defines character as moral excellence and firmness. Character means staying true to one's self. It entails moral correctness and yielding to conscience. A person of character would die doing the right thing.

Dr. Myles Munroe defined character as "dedication to a set of standards without wavering." He also said that character is when words, deeds, and actions are integrated.

So, this means that a leader who has character would be firm, morally excellent, and true to himself despite the circumstance. Speaking with character is having the ability or courage to say yes when you need to, and no when the situation demands it.

That is to say, a person of character would not compromise his standards. The quality of being true and unwavering which he possess, will give him the courage to do and say the right thing. He would call a spade a spade even if he's offered a million dollars to call it a machete.

Character is crucial for success in leadership. John C. Maxwell, on this, said, "your success stops where your character stops. You can never rise above the limitations of your character".

Many political leaders have compromised their standards. They have acted out of character probably because they were under pressure. Or, perhaps, they were offered money or power. For instance, some politicians agree on bad deals, they lie to their supporters, or wrongly decide to get support for their campaign.

Even noble career-people like lawyers have failed in character. For instance, a prominent Texas Judge, Rodolfo Delgado, aged 66, falls into this category. CNN headlines about this case ran thus: "A former texas judge is sentenced for accepting cash bribes stashed in beer boxes."

According to the U.S attorney's office (Texas southern district), Delgado "conspired with an attorney to accept bribes in exchange for favorable judicial consideration on criminal cases in his courtroom." Isn't this rather unfortunate? That a leader people trusted was engaged in such a lowering act? He was a leader people believed in. He could have said NO.

For a person to overcome such a great temptation, he or she would need courage—the kind that offshoots from soundness of character. According to Dr. Myles Munroe, "character is the foundation of leadership. This means that you can't be a great leader without a great character. A character that will enable you to say yes and no, without being influenced to compromise—such is a great character!

Are you a person of character? Do you have values that can help keep your words and actions in check? Or can you sell your soul for a morsel of bread? Your character is who you are. And will determine whether you stay true to yourself and your vision, despite the pressure or challenge.

HONESTY IS GOLD

"It takes strength and courage to admit the truth."

RICK RIORDAN

Previously, you saw that a great leader is a person who can say yes when he needs to and no when the situation demands it, without making promises he can't keep. Permit me to add – even when the going gets tough! In this part, we'll discuss honesty.

Honesty is a character trait. It is the quality of being straightforward, truthful, and sincere. It also means to be genuine and trustworthy. Honesty reflects strength. Why do I say this? So many people are dishonest because they don't want to seem weak or ignorant. They can't stand being seen for who they truly are. They exalt other people's opinions about them, above their peace of mind.

Are you guilty, friend? People have said they are rich when they're broke. Posed with cars that aren't theirs, lived in houses they couldn't afford. Some people claim the abilities they don't have. They are not honest, and this, mainly, is a sign of weakness. An honest person knows his worth and value. He doesn't need other people's opinions to be happy or fulfilled. Such a person derives his happiness and fulfillment from his character. He lives by sets of values that reflects who he is. He doesn't need an outward definition of himself.

Therefore, he doesn't venture to impress others. This kind of leader is not a people- pleaser but a vision-achiever. If sincerity will make him look weak, he's happy to accept it. If having integrity means that people won't like him, he's okay with it. If being truthful means that an opportunity will be lost, let it happen.

Are you an honest person? Honesty will make you a great leader because you'll be trusted. And remember, influence is a manifestation of earned trust.

Dr. Myles Munroe said, "Never say honesty is your best policy, for this will mean you have a third and a fourth-best. A person of character will say, that's my only policy". Brian Tracy said, "Having honesty and integrity in the workplace is one of the most important qualities of great leadership." He also stressed that these two qualities are the foundation of real leadership. Therefore, good leaders defend their integrity and stick to what is right.

Even in the home, many fathers have failed in honesty. Over and over, consistently broken promises live children disillusioned, and trust no longer comes easy. For instance, a dad promises to attend his son's basketball game but fails to make good his promise. Or, he misses his daughter's recital after getting her hopes up.

Along the line, resentment and mistrust set in, and such a father loses confidence with his kids. Honesty has tremendous effects on a leader's self-esteem. Don't give up on it.

You can't be effective as a leader if your words can't be trusted. Therefore, honesty in your dealings with others is a necessity. Randy Conley has this to say about honesty "telling the truth is at the core of being honest, but it's not the only behavior that people interpret as honesty. Sharing information openly, not coloring or hiding parts of the truth to fit an agenda, and delivering tough news with tact and diplomacy all go into someone forming a perception of you as an honest leader".

We've got to learn these things and apply them to our lives. If you could find character in a chest of treasures, honesty would be gold. Remember, only an honest leader would have the courage to say YES when he needs to, and NO when the situation demands it, without making promises he can't keep. Come on. Let's consider Joseph's character.

JOSEPH: A MAN OF CHARACTER WHO REFUSED TO COMPROMISE.

All aspiring leaders have a thing or two to learn from Joseph. Popularly known as "Joseph, the dreamer." As a young Hebrew boy, he was loved by his father, hated by his brothers and betrayed. God gave Joseph great dreams about his destiny, and often, he would share them with his family.

His ten elder brothers hated him for his dream and vision. They conspired against him and sold him to slave dealers, who sold him to an Egyptian captain named Potiphar.

While in his Egyptian master's house. Joseph conducted himself honorably. Soon, he became prosperous. Think about it! He was a slave, yet a prosperous man, for his master, saw that God's grace was upon him. And that God caused all he did to prosper. Joseph attended to his duties with diligence. Therefore, he made him overseer of his whole house.

69

Consider that Joseph was a Hebrew, not an Egyptian. Remember that his master had other servants before Joseph. Yet, he chose to put him in charge. What do you think distinguished him? What made him so trustworthy? One word; character.

There is a swagger and beauty that comes from charisma. But then there is a confidence which comes from strength of character. The lion moves with grace because of its personality and inner strength. This was Joseph's case.

However, a day came when this young Hebrew boy would have to prove what stuff he was made of. The Bible reveals that his master's wife was a lustful woman. She set her sights on the young man and desired to sleep with him. Genesis 39:7 says, "And it came to pass after these things, that his master's wife cast her eyes upon Joseph; and she said, "Lie with me."

Now you've got to understand. Her husband was a great man in Egypt. He was Potiphar, captain of the King's armies. She had the power to make Joseph great and increase his status. And I bet she was a beautiful woman. This invitation must have been inviting, or was it?

Think about it for just a moment. If you were in Joseph's shoes, what would you have done?

Guess what Joseph did. According to Genesis 39:8, **HE REFUSED**. He said **NO**, he spoke with character and honesty.

How did Joseph exhibit the courage to say no when he needed to?

1. He valued the trust and responsibility of leadership.

Joseph's answer to his master's wife reflects the integrity of his heart. How many men would have jumped at such an opportunity? Thousands! But Joseph wasn't enticed in the least. He refused. "With me in charge," he told her, "my master does not concern himself with anything in the house; everything he owns, he has entrusted into my care. No one is greater in this house than I am. My master has withheld nothing from me except you because you are his wife. How then could i do such a wicked thing and sin against God.

From the scripture above, it is clear what Joseph was valued above all else. He had earned the trust of his master via responsibility. He saw not living up to Potiphar's expectation and breaching his trust as a wicked act. Therefore, he dared to say no.

What about you? Have you accepted an offer you should have turned down? Do you value trust? Leaders who put a high price on trust, will be less prone to breaking it, either by word or deed.

Friend, learn from Joseph today. Character is the willingness to choose principles over pleasure. Just like Joseph, you can say NO at the right time.

2. He was committed to God and his vision

Another thing that strengthened Joseph to say NO was his vision and commitment to God. Remember that Egypt was a gentile nation. The people didn't worship the God of the Hebrews. Yet his master perceived that God was with him. The only logical explanation is that Joseph's commitment to God was evident to all. His lifestyle and conduct reflected his religion. Can people say this about you?

Also, he was committed to his vision. Aforetime, God had given him pictures of his future. And although Joseph was prosperous, he knew that the vision hadn't come to pass yet. He saw his family bowing before him in his dreams that was yet to happen. So his vision kept him constrained. It demanded focus and discipline. "Where there is no vision, the people cast off restraint…"[3]

He knew he still had a long way to go. And neither Potiphar nor his wife could make his dream come true. It was God-given, so it would be perfected by God.

---

[3] Proverbs Chapter 29 Verse 18 (BSB)

Staying true to God and your vision will help your character. It'll guarantee your success as a leader. What's more, it will give you the courage to say NO when you need to.

JUDAH: A LEADER WHO EXHIBITED A LACK OF CHARACTER AND HONESTY

The best lessons learned are from failures. But it shouldn't be *your* failure.

An example of dishonesty in a leader and its consequence is Judah, the fourth son of Jacob. .Judah left his father's house to make his own home. He got married to his wife, Shuah, and God blessed them with children. These were three male children called Er, Onan, and Shelah. Overtime, Judah's first son Er, got married to a woman named Tamar. But he didn't live long. Er was an evil man, so God killed him.

After losing Er, Judah asked his second son Onan to marry Tamar so she could bare seed for her husband. Now, in that era, this was part of the duty of a brother-in-law. Can you imagine that? Well, God also killed Onan because, although he slept with Tamar, he got rid of his sperm so she wouldn't get pregnant. He didn't want to perform his duty and prolong his brother's lineage.

At this point, Judah had lost two sons. He was reluctant to let Shelah marry Tamar because he feared that she was cursed. Moreover, he didn't want his last living son to die. So he sent her away to her father's house, asking her to remain a widow until Shelah was of age.

Judah was making a promise he couldn't keep. He knew he would not let Shelah marry Tamar. He probably made the promise because he didn't want to be called a wicked man, otherwise, he would not hurt Tamar's feelings. But he wasn't honest with her.

This event was the first sign of the crack in Judah's character. Most people try to blame their bad actions on their circumstances. But, in reality, the pressure only forces out what is inside of us. Oranges produce orange juice when squeezed.

After a while, Judah grew old; his wife died, and he felt lonely. One day, on his way to visit his sheepshearers, he saw a woman standing along the road. She stood dressed as a prostitute, and he asked her to go to bed with him. Since he didn't have money to pay her with, the woman asked him for some items as a pledge, so that he would return to pay her.

The woman asked for Judah's symbols of authority. His staff, signet ring, and bracelets! The shocking thing is, he agreed to give them to her. Sensibly, this should have been a sign to call it quits, to "snap back to reality." But he never did. He was a man who lacked character and honesty, and had met his kind.

Little did he know that this woman was his daughter-in-law in disguise. Tamar had perceived his deceit. She noticed that her father-in-law had not kept his promise. She was desperate; therefore, she hatched an equally deceitful plan; she'll get her husband's father to impregnate her.

However, this tragedy wouldn't have happened if Judah had spoken with character and integrity; if he had kept to his word. Pitiably, he didn't have the courage to say No when he needed to.

SHADRACH, MESHACH, AND ABEDNEGO: MEN WHO HAD THE COURAGE TO SAY "NO"

The King of Babylon, Nebuchadnezzar, was a powerful man. But an idol worshipper. He made an idol of gold, which was 90 feet tall and 9 feet wide. And commanded all his subjects in all the provinces to bow down and worship it. Anyone who rebelled against this order would be thrown into a furnace of fire.

Nevertheless, there lived in Babylon, Jews captured from Israel. Among them were Shadrach, Meshach, and Abednego. These three were pious men who feared God greatly. They heard the royal decree but refused to bow down and worship the golden idol. The law of their God prohibited the worship of any other god or image. They decided to be unwavering.

They were reported to the King and brought before him. The King gave the three a choice. They either bow before the image or cast in the raging fire furnace. Their answer to the king I believe is one of the greatest examples of courage, bravery, and unwavering character in the face of danger;

"Shadrach, Meshach, and Abednego answered the king, O Nebuchadnezzar, it is not necessary for us to answer you on this point."[4]

Wow! What courage! These men would rather die for their principles than save their necks. They trusted in God because they knew Him. And they feared Him more than the King. To do what they did, one has to be a person of character, know God, and fear Him.

JESUS: AN ENIGMA OF BOTH CHARACTER AND HONESTY

Joseph is a man to follow. Judah is a leader to learn from. The three courageous Hebrews are worth emulating. But there's a leader whose style of life is flawless. He is Jesus. He is the greatest leader that ever walk the face of this earth. His record is unbeatable. His standards are high, yet you can "take His yoke on yourself and learn of Him."

Jesus was a powerful and influential leader. He was the most famous man in his time. And still is! Yet, He described Himself as "meek and lowly in heart." What a conundrum!

He was an enigma of both character and honesty. He stuck to his vision and didn't value the praise of me. He was hated for his honesty and simplicity. Once, Jesus so impressed a multitude that they wanted to make Him King, but He ran away.

How did Jesus speak with character and honesty?

1. Jesus refused to change his message

The religious leaders of Jesus' day hated his message and everything he did. Countless times, they attempted to entrap him with his own words so they could arrest him. Not only this, but they also wanted him dead.

---

[4] Daniel Chapter 3 Verse 16 (AMPC BIBLE)

Jesus knew all this but was never scared or pressured into watering down his message.

Jesus couldn't preach the Kingdom and repentance without revealing that He was the Son of God; the peace offering, the lamb of God that takes away the sins of the world. His boldness, however, infuriated the Jewish leaders;

"For this reason, they tried all the more to kill him; not only was he breaking the Sabbath, but He was even calling God His own Father, making Himself equal with God."[5]

Jesus faced a lot of opposition and had threats to his life. Yet he had enough character to help him stay true to His vision. In john 6:38, as an expression of His unwavering commitment to vision, he said that He came to do the will of the Father who sent Him, and not His own".

2. Jesus always had courage to speak the truth

In Luke 13:31-35, some Pharisees came to Jesus, urging Him to run away because Herod wanted to kill Him. They implied that Jesus should quit His ministry. He was casting out demons and healing this sick, so his influence continued to increase. Probably, Herod believed Jesus wanted His throne and felt threatened.

However, before this time, Herod had beheaded John the Baptist. So, Jesus should have been terrified. The men who brought Him the news expected Him to take to His heels. Little did they know that; courage loves to laugh in the face of danger. And honesty is addicted to dying for the right course.

Jesus said to them in verse 32, "Go and tell that fox, 'I will keep on driving out demons and healing people today and tomorrow, and on the third day I will reach my goal.'"

He would not compromise for whatsoever reason. He had the courage to bear the consequence of staying true and standing up for what He believed in.

---

[5] John Chapter 5 Verse 18 (NIV BIBLE)

3. Jesus didn't make fake promises

Jesus was a great leader because he made no fake promises. He didn't need to. Jesus always has the capacity to do what he ought to do. But when his vision or timing constrained him, he had to courage to say YES when he needed to, and NO when the situation demanded it. He always made sure He could do what He said, ensuring that it was in line with His vision.

In Mark 7:26, a Gentile woman came to Jesus. She fell and cried at his feet. Her daughter was possessed with a devil, and she desired that Jesus would heal her. However, Jesus declined. He was a man known for His compassion, yet he wasn't worried about what people would say.

His reason was that it was outside his vision. He told the woman. His ministry was to people of Israel alone and gentiles. Therefore, on these grounds, He couldn't help her. This was Jesus being honest and not making promises He couldn't keep.

Although He later healed her daughter because her faith moved the Hand of God; however, He cared more about character and honesty than being liked or appreciated.

Can you do what Jesus did? What if your life gets threatened? Do you think that being honest will make you lose your supporters? Would you rather stay true to your vision, or be given to treachery? In times when you have to choose between principles and pleasure, what would it be?

Learn from Jesus today and gain the courage to say YES when you need to, and NO when the situation demands it.

Finally, Great Leaders Deliberately Win Trust

"BELIEVE ALSO IN ME"

Jesus knew the importance of saying the right thing. He knew that trust was essential to his vision as a leader. People only follow who they can rely on. Jesus knew this, so He was intentional about winning trust.

If you become intentional about trust, you would find the courage to stay true to your words and avoid making promises you can't keep. An example of Jesus' purposefulness in building trust can be seen in John 14:1 where he said, "Let not your heart be troubled: **ye believe in god, believe also in me**. In my Father's house are many mansions: if it were not so, I would have told you. I go to prepare a place for you".

Can you see how Jesus intentionally established trust? He made sure that he deserved it. He explained that if His words weren't true He wouldn't have said them. He meant what He said, and he said what He meant.

My dear friend, take a leaf out of Jesus's book. Go for the trust! How can you do this? Learn to always speak with character and honesty. Have a consistent character, whether in secret or the open. Be courageous enough to answer your conscience in all kinds of situations. Great leaders dare to say YES when they need to, and NO when the situation demands it. Be the leader whose word can be taken to the bank.

LESSON 6

A LISTENING EAR AND A HEART OF EMPATHY

It takes a great man to be a good listener

Calvin Coolidge

Can you fix a problem you don't know about? How can you lead people you don't understand? Is it possible to understand people you don't know? Have you ever wondered why God said, those who show mercy will also obtain the same? Think about how bizarre the world would be without the sense of hearing and feeling. Mind-numbing right?

Along with the sense of listening, a great leader has one other quality to harmonize his or her sense of listening for effectiveness— a heart of empathy. One thing that every leader must keep in mind is that leadership is not about you. Rather, it is about serving other people to the best of your ability. In fact, the Lord Jesus Christ, the greatest leader that ever lived, emphasized this truth.

When his disciples had a quarrel amongst themselves over who was the greatest, Jesus gave them a lesson on leadership. He told them that He did not come to be served, but to serve others and to give His life for many. Matthew 20: 28 (MSG) says, "That is what the Son of Man has done: He came to serve, not to be served and then to give away his life in exchange for the many who are held, hostage."

Think about this for a moment. This means that a leader is for the people he leads; leadership is about the people being led, and not about the leader. Therefore, anything and everything that the leader thinks, says, or does is not for himself, but for the people being led. The skills of a leader are not about the leader; if the leader does not have the skills that benefit the people he leads, then his skills are useless as long as the leadership is concerned. For this reason, the leader must develop skills that benefit the people who are being led, and not even himself. Two of the very important leadership skills are addressed in this chapter.

In Matthew 20 verse 28 above, you will see that in the stead of demanding that others attend to His needs, Jesus was concerned about their needs. If this is not the greatest example of leadership, then nothing is. Jesus never once talked about what they could do for him or even what he could do for himself. He committed to making their lives better, and that is what a leader does. Leaders commit themselves to improve other people's lives.

Now, we know that leadership is about serving people, which is akin to giving people what they need, but how can you know what people need? How do you think that Jesus was able to accomplish His mission? How can you know what people need in order to give it to them? Listening!

Jesus was never too busy to listen to the people he led. In fact, he always asked them a lot of questions. In John chapter 5 from verses 1 to 5, we see how much attention Jesus gave to knowing what the people wanted. He did not just go ahead and do what he knew he could do, or what he felt that a person or people needed.

Jesus met a crippled man by the pool of Bethesda. That man had been unwell for 38 whole years, and he had sat by the pool for almost as long waiting for somebody to help him into the healing waters at the time when it was stirred by the angel of God. The man had no one to help him, and without help, he would have been there all his life he would have died right there, waiting for help from someone who could get him into the pool at exactly the right time. Is it not obvious that the man needed to be healed? Even a person who does not know not anything about the healing pool or about how long the man had been there would just take a look at the crippled man, sitting there crippled and old, and the person would know right away that what he needed was to be healed.

Yet, wait for it, Jesus asked him, "Do you want to get well?"

Even the man must have been incredulous. Was it not obvious that he wanted to get well? Yet, Jesus inquired; He did not make assumptions. Jesus asked to know if the man wanted to be well, giving him an opportunity to express himself. By this, he further proved that he came for the people, and nothing he was doing was for or about himself. He asked them what they wanted because he knew that his power was for them, and not for himself.

Can you imagine this?

Can you picture a leader who asks people which way they want to go before leading them, even though it is obvious that they want to go the same way that he does? It takes a lot to be this kind of leader; it takes a listening ear, and it takes an empathetic heart to know what a person wants and to understand what a person is going through. The way that Jesus led while in the flesh, and His position in heaven (as our high priest) is the same way leaders need to know that their skills are not for themselves, but for the people who follow them.

This is the attitude of a great leader; sadly, this virtue is still a rare commodity in our world today. Several of the supposed leaders today feel that they are an asset to their followers, and while this is true, this attitude does not allow them to lead people the right way. You know, this is why many of the leaders today are more like rulers than people who can be considered leaders. Most of the time, when leaders lead people in this way, they may think that they are leading people because they are moving forward. However, they may later discover that they have only been walking alone or dragging very unwilling people along the road. This is not true leadership. Let's keep going to find out how to employ these skills effectively.

Listening is not a walk in the park

We have two ears and one mouth, so we should listen more than we say.

Zeno of Citium

Have you ever sat through a whole lecture or even a sermon, and at the end of it, you discover that you have no idea what has been said? This actually happens more times than you can imagine.

Have you ever spent a lot of time and effort to talk to someone else, and they ended up misinterpreting your own words? Or maybe you even had an interesting conversation that could have been considered to be heated up and interactive, but afterward, you couldn't remember what it was about? Or are you like some people I know, and you forget a person's name five seconds after you heard it?

The truth is that listening is really not as simple as it is made to look, but it is still very important. We don't learn about listening at school; no school teaches a course or subject titled, "The Art of Listening." Or is there?

Rather, we are taught to read, and it is quickly assumed that a person who is a good reader would also be a good listener, but this isn't true. Listening and reading are not at all alike.

Even more, the people who believe that good readers are also good listeners forget that in the real world, we talk and listen more than we read. Importantly, listening to bosses, colleagues, teammates, partners, and others contribute to determining how successful we would turn out to be. Consequently, the inability to listen just might bring about failure.

Research has revealed that the reason why listening is so hard is because of the speed of the human brain in processing thoughts. According to psychologists, we think faster than we talk. They also say that the average American says about 120 words per minute, and this is slow compared to how fast we think.

This means that when we listen to someone else speak, we try to slow down our brains in order to comprehend at the pace of the other person's speech. However, this is unnatural and quite difficult; it is even harder when you are not doing it consciously. It is believed that the brain attaches more words to every word we hear. Therefore, this means that we will tend to have more words in our minds from the conversation, aside from the ones communicated to us.

Have you ever listened to someone talk, and at the end of the talk, you discover that you have added a lot of words to what the person actually said? This actually happens a lot.

Also, the speed at which we think creates ample room for thoughts to stray now and again. Can you relate to this? Have you ever been in a classroom or in a congregation, yet you are a thousand miles away? Have you ever been somewhere, and from the hall where you are, you find that your thoughts have strayed to your kitchen or to the show you saw the night before? Our thoughts stray; a lot. It takes a conscious and purposeful attempt to pay real attention and listen to others.

Beyond the speed of our thought process, we humans really love to have people listen to us than we want to listen. We enjoy the exhilarating feeling of expressing ourselves to people who are paying attention. It gives us a sense of self-importance and prominence.

We must remind ourselves while having conversations and interactions that one cannot talk and listen at the same time. No wonder the Bible in James chapter 1 verse 19 says, "Wherefore my beloved brethren, let every man be swift to hear, slow to speak...". This may sound like an ordinary piece of advice from Apostle James to believers, but the truth is that he was letting us in on a vital skill. He was saying, in essence, "If you want to be great, be a good listener, and talk less."

 Have you noticed that the worst listeners are the same people who are talkative? Are you like that? As a leader, do you listen to understand, or do you listen just to reply? It was Steve R. Covey who observed that most people do not listen with the intent to understand; they listen with the intent to form a reply.

James was asking his audience to be swift to hear, to place more importance on hearing than on speaking. He wanted them to listen curiously, to pay attention and be interested in what other people are saying. This is because, naturally, we tend to value our opinions above the opinions of others, and so we unconsciously shut our ears to their words, sometimes only hearing what we want to hear. I put it to you that this is not listening.

Besides, the words **slow to speak** does not mean that we should talk slowly, or that we should all talk less. It really does mean that we should put listening to and understanding what other people are saying above, giving information. It implies a reluctance to dominate a conversation and the desire to learn. It means that we should hold ourselves back and resist the desire to do nothing but talk and expect all other people to listen, while we do not do the same.

Dear friend, every aspect of human life has something to do with associating and interacting with others; this necessitates communication and, consequently, conversations. Conversations do not happen unless the interlocutors involved are passing and receiving the message of the conversation. This means that a conversation has not happened if only one person talks, and the other person only listens. There must be turn-taking to get the best out of any conversation.

True conversations are even more important for leaders. Can two work together except they agree? Now, tell me, can two people agree if they do not listen to one another? How do you know that you are on the same page with the people you are leading? You must learn to do more than just talk to the people you are leading about where you are going; you have to also listen to them talk about where you are going together.

This means that if we want to be happy, successful, and efficient leaders with happy and progressive followers, we must learn to listen to others. As difficult as it is to listen, leaders must learn to do so. Listening is a skill that must be cultivated to facilitate in anything you do effectively; parenting, building a relationship, teaching, and, most importantly, leading.

How much do you care?

Nobody cares how much you know, until they know how much you care.

Theodore Roosevelt

Have you ever noticed how much attention people give to babies? They can't talk intelligibly, yet when they make any sounds, everyone is interested and pays attention. Everyone will want to understand a baby's needs and offer to meet them. Why do we act like this? It is because we care about the babies. We know that they cannot help themselves, so we are ready to help them in whatever way we can. Now, because we care about them and want to help them, we listen for their complaints and their giggles. The giggles tell us that we are doing pretty well with caring for them, and the crying tells us that there is something that we need to do; this is why we pay attention because we want to fill their needs.

This is what a true leader does. A true leader cares about his or her followers and knows that every peep or murmur from them means something, and so, to care for followers properly, true leaders pay attention to every word that comes out of their followers because it will help them to lead better.

As a leader, Jesus exhibited a great level of care and concern for His followers. The Bible says that Jesus looked at the multitude that followed Him, and He saw that they were as harassed as sheep without a shepherd. From the way he treated them, paying attention, and reacting accordingly when he saw that they were hungry and tired, we can see that he was compassionate towards them. The leadership of Jesus was not about Himself and His vision alone. It was about others.

When the multitude was tired and hungry in Matthew chapter 15, verse 32, the people did not call him and tell him. He noticed this by himself because he was paying attention, and because he was listening to them, the people he was leading, and the people he cared for. How would he have known they were tired if he had just been going about the business of declaring his thoughts? Those people indeed needed to hear his voice, but they also needed to eat and rest, and Jesus got to know this by listening. Most importantly, Jesus was listening because he cared, and because of that, he was able to lead them in the right way.

In Mark chapter 10, there is quite an intriguing story of a blind man whose name was stated to be Timaeus Bartimaeus. This man daily sat at the highway of Jericho, begging for alms, but on a miracle-tinged afternoon, he wanted something better than alms. While he was sitting at his usual position, hoping for the passing of generous people, he heard the sound of an excited crowd. What was causing these folks to buzz like bees, he probably wondered. Bartimaeus must have asked the people around him, "Hey! What is going on? What is that noise?" He got the marvelous information that Jesus, the highly acclaimed miracle worker, was passing by. What wonderful news!

When he was told that Jesus was passing by, he began to call to Him for mercy. He had heard about Jesus, the healer, and this Jesus had something he wanted badly. So, Bartimaeus, the blind man, cried out loudly, "Thou son of David have mercy on me!"

Sadly, it seemed that he was seeking for mercy from too far away a distance because the people around him turned out to be quite mean. They told him to be quiet. The actions of those people around him reflect the self-importance of the average human being. They had no concern for the blind man beside them who most definitely needed to receive his sight. They kept on trying to quiet him down. They must have felt that such a busy and important man, such as Jesus, must have a lot of prominent people and important issues to deal with, and so he should not have time for beggars like Bartimaeus. Can you blame them? Most leaders today are selective about who they advise because they only take time to hear from the "**important**" people. Even at that, the man would not be stopped. He continued to cry out for his salvation until Jesus Christ finally heard him. That day, Jesus proved to everyone that in leadership, every single one of the followers is important.

As soon as Jesus (God in flesh) heard him, He stood still and asked for the blind and lowly beggar be brought forward to him. Jesus Christ of Nazareth, the most sought after miracle worker, listened to the poor beggar. What a fascinating turn of events! Apparently, Jesus, the great healer, did not seem to think that He was too busy or too important to have a conversation with a beggar. Instead, He acted like he had all the time in the world. All the time for a beggar? He acted as though Bartimaeus was the only one he needed to listen to, out of the throngs of people around him. If you think that this is remarkable, what He did next will dazzle you. Jesus asked Timaeus Bartimaeus, "What do you want? How can I help you today?"

"'What can I do for you?'" Jesus said"- Mark 10:51 (MSG)

Jesus was willing to listen to this man and solve his problem. He cared for him, and so he wanted to know his problems and fix them, but he needed to know what the problems were. Can you now see that caring for people and listening to them goes hand in hand? Jesus did not just assume the problem and start to offer advice. We all know that Jesus could have figured out what the problem was, but rather than show off his powers of discernment, he asked and listened. He may not have had the time to listen patiently, after all, there were a lot of people around him waiting for him to get to them; yet, he did, he listened.

When you think about being a great leader, what do you think about? Massive success? Inspiring people with your words? Influencing people to do the right thing by telling them what to do? The chance to be separated from the crowd and have everyone listen to your words with rapt attention? Did you think about serving other people? Did you think about becoming a confidante? Did you think about listening to the people you lead and solving their problems? Or are you the kind of leader who is just too busy to care and too distracted to listen?

In Jesus' leadership, it always seemed as though he had all the time in the world for others. A great leader cares about those he leads. As a leader, when you listen to one person, you should pay attention, and listen as though the person is the only one you need to be paying attention to at that time. The people who followed Jesus chased after Him because they knew He cared, and they could not get enough of it. Everyone likes to be cared for, and what better way to show a person that you care about them than to pay attention to the things that they are saying. Yes! How much do you care?

Listening is the first step in problem-solving

Can you imagine a policeman who arrives at a crime scene and does not ask questions? Or even one who asks questions, but does not pay attention to what eyewitnesses are telling him. Even with the greatest intuitive skills, this policeman would be missing out on a lot of information. With so much information missing, how can he solve the crime?

How can you fix a problem that you do not really know about? You cannot. Do you want to be a great leader? Then you've got to know something vital. The greatest leaders that ever lived were problem solvers. They lived to make life easier for others. All the great inventions are the response of great leaders to the needs of others. Even Jesus was a problem solver. He came to reconcile humanity back to God.

How does listening come in? I'll tell you but first answer this question. Have you ever had a friend who was sad yet he/she wouldn't open up to you? Were you able to help them? I'm sure your answer is no. That's how listening comes in. When you can listen and understand what others are going through, then you'll be able to help them. Assuming you know what people want will only cause problems.

This means you must be determined to be a problem solver by listening patiently to others. If you listen to people, you'll discover that you can solve their problems. An example of a great leader in the Bible who was concerned with solving problems and listening to others was Joseph, the son of Jacob.

Joseph was framed by his master's wife and thrown into prison. While in prison, the warden put him in charge of all the affairs of the prison. As time went on, some of Pharaoh's officials (the chief butler and baker) offended him, and he threw them into prison. This was the same prison in which Joseph was overseer.

On a certain day, Pharaoh's officials were downcast, and Joseph noticed. You have to take into consideration the fact that Joseph had his problems. He had been betrayed by his brothers, sold into slavery, accused falsely, and thrown into prison. He was in a strange land and didn't know what was going to happen to his hopes and dreams. Yet, even though Joseph was the one in need of help, he could still notice the needs of others.

So on seeing their sad expressions, Joseph approached the chief butler and baker to listen to them. He asked them what the problem was and discovered that both men had had dreams they couldn't interpret. Their major problem at that point was; they had nobody to tell them what their dreams meant. Well, coincidentally, after listening to them, Joseph had just what they needed. He could interpret their dreams, which he did and solved their problem.

You see, to listen to others and keep quiet enough to understand them remains a difficult task, especially when you have your problems. But great leaders learn to master the skill of listening so that they can help those in need. So would you rather be self-centered or a great leader? Have you responded to people wrongly when they tried to confide in you? Do you let your mood affect your ability to listen? Well, you can learn from Joseph today.

Can I wear your shoes?

Friend, I believe you've enjoyed our discussion up to this point. We've been talking about listening, but I believe now is the right time to bring in the subject of empathy. Have you lost a loved one? Or you know someone who has? Well, what most people try to do when it comes to consoling someone who is grieving is to empathize with him/her. As a result, you hear words like, "I know what you're going through," "I know you're hurting."

According to the English dictionary, empathy means identification with or understanding of the thoughts, feelings, or emotional state of another person. It also means to put yourself in another person's shoes.

This is an indispensable ingredient for great leadership. Some people are able to listen, but because they are unable to relate to the other person's experience, they still behave like they didn't hear a word. For example, King Solomon was a good listener. Even though he was known as a wise king, who walked in balance, justice, and equity, yet he had more than those. Yes! His wisdom was mixed with empathy!

A strange case was brought before the wise King. It involved two women, one dead and one loving child. Both women claimed the living child as hers. Apparently, one had slept over hers at night and killed it. But how on earth would anyone know which of the women was lying? For the wise King, it was a matter of empathy. He had an idea.

He put himself in a mother's shoes. What would a mother do to protect her child? How would she react if her child's life hung in the balance? Once the King recovered from his musings, he asked the child to be divided equally between the women.

What happened next thrilled the audience gathered in the throne room. The real mother cried for mercy, asking the child to be given to the other and spared. While the woman who lied insisted that the child be divided. King Solomon had solved the case. He had revealed the true mother. But how did he do it? He put himself in the mother's shoes.

So you see friend, the King didn't just have a listening ear, he also had a heart of empathy. How many times have you failed to treat people right because you didn't take the time to put yourself in their situation? Would you also come late to work if your child fell ill in the morning?

Great leaders do not compromise. They don't replace efficiency with excuses, but they always have time to listen and to understand what others are going through. To show empathy as a leader will show those who look up to you that you care about them.

Even when God desired to save the world from their sins, He didn't send one who couldn't understand human frailties and weakness. He sent His only begotten son Jesus who was equal in every way like God. And Jesus came in the form of man so that he would be a savior who was acquainted with our shortcomings and able to show mercy.

Putting yourself in other people's shoes should be your default state as a leader. You should be able to cry, laugh, and mourn with others. Truly, if leadership is about others, then empathy is a sure path to success and greatness. If this principle guides your decisions as a leader, you'll find yourself making wiser decisions.

How empathetic in heart are you as a leader? Are you able to put yourself in other people's positions? Or have you been very critical on others because of the lack of this virtue/ lack of empathy would make us downright mean? I'll show you people who neglected empathy and were as mean as vultures.

Do you remember the story of a lady who was caught in the act of adultery and was to be stoned to death? Fortunately, the Jews took this matter to Jesus to Judge. They expected Him to succumb to their verdict because it was indeed lawful. But what did Jesus do? Let me put it like this. He passed the lady's shoes around.

Jesus told the men who held their stones high above their heads, ready to execute judgment; "He who is without sin should cast the first stone." With this statement, Jesus causes them to put themselves in the woman's place. All those men realized that they were guilty of the same sin and equally worthy of death

Think about this, friend. Consider the cruelty of these men. Isn't it so easy to be hard on others? Do you realize that you excuse most of your failures as mistakes but regard others as lazy, wicked, or unproductive? This is why having a listening ear alone is not enough. Great leaders have a listening ear and a heart of empathy.

LESSON 7

VALUE FOR TEAMWORK

"None of us is as smart as all of us."

-Ken Blanchard

C onsider the legend of the Great Pyramid and the audacity of
the tower of Babel. How about the determination of the
NASA team that landed on the moon and the tenacity of the
Manhattan project research team that produced the first nuclear
weapons during World War 2? What if you witnessed the sync among
the team of chefs that work at big restaurants in Paris? Or the power
of the **UCLA's** dynasty that won seven consecutive national
championships from 1967 to 1973? Can we talk of greatness, legacy,
power and dominion without teamwork?

The truth is, life's chaos and complexity can be veiled by the
extraordinary beauty of harmonious interaction. The simplicity of
individualism breeds mediocrity and complexity can become chaos
when it lacks collaboration.

For instance, why do science call humans higher animals? The answer
is, unlike unicellular and other multicellular organisms, humans excel
all creation through an unbroken synergy of their complex body parts
with their higher cognitive and communication abilities. Likewise,
beyond the capacity of sole-proprietorship, coordinated, collaborative
and collective activities are required to yield greatness and abundance.

Welcome to another impactful phase of this volume. You are about to
discover the benefits and power of teamwork. I crave to help you come
to a place of utmost priority for teamwork. Like a car owner who
would not ignore a fault in any part of his car, you must get to work
on where you consider a defect on your team, you must work to make
your goals worth pursuing for your dreams to come true.

What is a Team?

I'll like to define a team as a group of people synergizing their skills, talents, knowledge, mutual support and resources to achieve effective results.

This definition shows that teamwork is all about adding up individuals' contribution to creating an outcome that increases at an exponential rate. By this I mean, when you add 1+1 in mathematics on individualistic formula, the result will be 2. But when collaboration and teamwork is in place, 1+1= 11 (Yes, I mean ELEVEN!), a difference of 9. How about 1+1+1, you shouldn't expect anything less than an exponential increase.

Teamwork is the lifeblood of a dream and the hope of a significant vision. Whatever you can do alone may not endure beyond your lifetime, but whatever is done with teamwork can become trans-generational! Therefore, your big dream is in the life-support system of your team members. How much of this have you realized? And how has this realization influenced your investment in team building?

John C. Maxwell, in his book, The 17 Indisputable Laws of Teamwork, said, "A great dream with a bad team is nothing more than a nightmare." Wow! It means nothing will work until your team works.

So, it is time to answer the big question: How much do I value teamwork? Whether you're a business leader, politician, engineer, religious leader, or single mother, I'll like to ask you the same question, are you co-operative, collaborative or competitive?

Remember the common saying, Two heads are better than one, it has nothing to do with the Siamese twins. This popular idiom implies that two minds can solve a problem more effectively than one. Or that the creativity of two always surpasses that of one. This statement has proven to be true since the beginning of time. How can we argue with it? Surprisingly, it seems to suggest that no matter how intelligent an individual is, he can't beat the power of two or more.

Think about this for a moment!

Friend, do you know that this truth didn't materialize out of thin air? No, it didn't. It was extracted from the greatest of all books – the Bible! Ecclesiastes 4:9 (GNT) says, "Two are better off than one because together they can work more effectively." Although the Bible didn't say two heads, it passes the same message. I believe that this bible verse preaches teamwork wonderfully. It audaciously states that two of anything (heads, hands, legs, etc.) is better than one.

Therefore, no matter how much a leader knows, he can't achieve much more outside his or her team. The world's most significant achievements aren't the work of lone rangers but team players. You have to ingrain this truth in your mind as a leader; an architect draws the plan for a house, but it is the builder who builds. Great leaders are those who value teamwork despite their vast knowledge.

Again, John C. Maxwell said, "Nothing of significance was ever achieved by an individual acting alone. Look below the surface, and you will find that all seemingly solo acts are really team efforts".

Of a truth, behind every great leader is a stanch team. Meaning, any boss or leader who aspires for greatness must do two things: quit the solo career and make teamwork a priority. John C. Maxwell had a lot to say on this subject, again he said, "For the person trying to do everything alone, the game really is over. If you want to do something big, you must link up with others. One is too small a number to achieve greatness. That's the law of significance."

Truth be told, smart alecks don't make great leaders. Great leaders are team leaders. Think about the benefits of teamwork: The fact that combined team resources are far higher, there is an increase in the probability of success, two hands get more work done faster. And together, everyone achieves more.

GOD IS A TEAM LEADER

"And God said, Let us make man…let them have dominion"

GENESIS 1:26

Creation is a proof of collaboration. It was neither a big-bang nor the gradual accident of billion years of evolution. God is the creator, but He wasn't alone. In the above scripture, God said, LET US!

Consider the greatness of God as portrayed by this popular hymn: HOW GREAT THOU ART. It is a song that conjures the greatness and magnificence of God. And it often brings to mind the infallibility of His wisdom. Our minds can't seem to exhaustively explore the truth that God is all-knowing, all-powerful and all-present.

Who is as wise as God? This is a question often asked in the scripture that doesn't require an answer. We all know that no one is as wise as God. God once asked Prophet Ezekiel a question in Ezekiel chapter 37 that required an all-knowing mind to give an appropriate answer. The smart Prophet recognized it as a trick-question and retorted, only you can answer that!

Although God has such vast knowledge, you'll discover that He is a team player. It may come as a shock to realize that God never does anything alone. Now, that isn't because He needs anyone. No, it's because it's His nature. Teamwork is the nature of God.

Have you ever heard of the word Trinity? I bet you have. It's one of the greatest and most popular doctrinal beliefs in Christianity—God in three persons. We believe that God is one, but He has revealed Himself in three personalities and dimensions to humanity. These three persons in one, are what is called the Godhead or trinity comprising of God the Father, God the Son, God the Holy Spirit.

The concept of the trinity is complex. No one completely understands it. It reveals that the three members of the Godhead are one. They function as a team. Yet, separately, they are all completely God in every way.

The Godhead exemplifies teamwork beautifully. Each member can exist alone, yet sustains oneness. Some theologians and Bible teachers believe that the Old Testament is the work of God the Father, the New Testament is the work of God the Son, and this present dispensation is the work of God the Holy Spirit.

Even in creation, you will see God working as a team. God, in Genesis 1:26, said, "Let us make man." First of all, you have to remember that God is the creator of the universe. The Bible doesn't talk about any other. Nevertheless, God was clearly seeking the input and collective efforts of other individuals in the Godhead. This was one of the first revelations of the Trinity, for all three members took part in the creation.

God is not just an individual. The Bible teaches something vital: God the Father, is the same as God the Son. And God the Holy Spirit is the same as the other two. Their will is one, their nature is one, and they are united. But the greatest implication of this truth is, God is a team player.

Now, we have been able to glean enough light that teaches us two things: God is a team, and God is a team player. He is such a team player that, He not only worked as a team to create man, He created man because He wanted to team up with man. Also in verse 26 of Genesis chapter one, He said, "Let them have dominion..." God didn't want to do everything by Himself.

Despite His infallibility and wisdom, He desired the input of someone else. His nature is teamwork. While He took care of matters in Heaven, He wanted a team to handle earthly affairs. So, He gave man dominion over everything he created, making him a partner.

Wow! Think about this for a moment. Let it sink in. God is the most successful leader in all eternity; because He achieves things through a team effort. He never does anything in heaven without His heavenly team – the Godhead. And He never does anything on earth without the involvement of man.

Do you remember when God was to destroy Sodom and Gomorrah for their wickedness? What did He say about doing the job? In Genesis 18:17, "Then the LORD said, "Shall I hide from Abraham what I am about to do?" Just imagine what God said! He didn't need Abraham in terms of wisdom or power. But it's His nature to work with a team. If you read the whole verse, you'll be amazed that God let Abraham influence His actions.

Lastly, there was this formidable team in the Bible, I call them, the tower of babel team. Scripture reveals these people had one language and one goal. They desired to build a city tall enough to reach heaven so that they could become famous. God wasn't excited about their vision. It was selfish and excluded Him. So He decided to disrupt their plans.

However, he commended them for something. God valued teamwork so much that He said, and I paraphrase, "these people are one; they are the dream team. Nothing will be impossible for them to achieve".

Friend, if God can be a team player, then you can be one too. Great leaders are team players.

THINK LIKE A COACH

"Don't aspire to be the best on the team. Aspire to be the best for the team"

Brian Tracy

We have lots of essential facts about coaches, especially football coaches. But one crucial similarity about every coach is, they don't play in a game. You don't see them getting all the glory, they are content with the success of the team.

A football player can dream of becoming the world's best. He can pursue a scoring number of goals in a season. He has the liberty to desire fame and glory for himself. But a coach's dream is for the team.

So many leaders, bosses and CEO's, make the mistake of thinking like one of the players. They want all the accolades and be the only ones scoring the goals, bringing the best ideas. They want to be recognized as the best. However, a team doesn't thrive on its leader's strength; every single member fuels it.

Football coaches seem to know this truth. No matter how knowledgeable a coach is of the game, you don't see him on the field. His goal is the success of the whole team. He wants the glory for the team. He wants to win, but not at the detriment of the team. This means that a coach spends time, training and building the skills of his players.

Hence, a leader ought to think like a coach not like one of the players. Many coaches were once great footballers. But once they became coaches, they stop to think about themselves and start to think for the team. It was John C. Maxwell, who said, "A sign of great team leader is the proper placement of people."

As a leader, you must know that every individual and their peculiarity is important to your team. So, you have to dedicate yourself to harnessing their potentials and helping them achieve more. Learn about their strengths and weaknesses to know how best it can be used for the achievement of a collective goal.

A coach values winning the game more than personal victories. A player can be satisfied with a medal without winning the championship. But a great leader wants the championship. Besides, thinking like a coach will help you see your team in a new light. A coach doesn't just care about winning. He cares about individuals first. He wants them to be the best, so he doesn't put his desires before the team's success.

TEAMWORK, DREAM WORK

"Unity is strength…when there are teamwork and collaboration, wonderful things can be achieved."

Mattie Stepanek

TOGETHER EVERYBODY ACHIEVES MORE, the most popular team backronym, is a statement more profound than it appears. A team is so powerful. A bunch of people effectively working together can achieve things others have tagged impossible. Just imagine Noah building the ark without the help of his family? Building an ark large enough to contain a pair of every animal species in the world was impossible, but a team of builders made it possible.

The easiest way to perform the most difficult task in the world, is to get a team. All over the scripture, you'll find relevant wisdom that teaches the power of teamwork. The Bible says that "one will chase a thousand, but two will chase ten thousand." Tell me, what kind of math was done here? My answer is team-mathematics.

Teamwork makes room for innovation, creativity, collaboration, and growth. On your journey to becoming a great leader, you need to carry with you the mindset of teamwork. It will be to you what water is to a man stuck in the desert.

Here are some truths on the importance of teamwork:

a. Teamwork involves more people and as a leader, you must always work with a team. Teams involve more hands, more ideas and support. When people work together, they get things done faster. For instance, an idea someone comes up with, will be properly checked by another for loopholes, thereby, becoming more effective. When a member of the team is weak, another can fill in for him/her. Also, one person's weakness is another person's strength. This means that a team has fewer limitations than one person.

b. Teamwork improves the leader; having value for teamwork is one of the best things that can happen to a leader. It was Albert Einstein who said and I paraphrase, if you try to make a fish climb a tree, you'll think it's not smart. As a leader, if you try to do everything yourself, you'll fail. Many times you'll feel like a fish trying to climb a tree. Teamwork helps leaders maximize their potentials and helps minimize their weaknesses. This is because he/she would have delegated that weakness to a member of the team who has strength in that area.

c. Teams are important because it provides room for different perspectives which make problem-solving easier.

d. Teamwork splits everything among team members. As a leader, you won't have to bear the responsibility alone. You and your team share profits or losses.

e. Teamwork is an important factor when it comes to staying focused. Working with other people will keep you accountable for the vision. Since your team will be looking up to you for direction and inspiration, you'll have to stay on top of your game.

MOSES: THE LONE RANGER WHO LEARNT THE HARD WAY

Life loves to be a teacher. But we don't only learn from good examples, do we? We can also learn a lot from people's mistakes. Moses was a leader in the bible who made a mistake in terms of teamwork but he later learned his lesson.

Exodus chapter 18 tells us of Jethro's visit while the Israelites were in the wilderness. Moses had sent his wife and kids back to his father-in-law in Midian. Although the reason for this is unclear, some Hebrew scholars believe that Moses had been advised by Aaron to send his family back, so as not to make them partake of the suffering in Egypt.

When Moses's father-in-law came to see Him, He shared with Jethro all the marvelous things God had done for them. However, while Jethro stayed with the Israelites for a while, he noticed a fault in his son-in-law's leadership style.

He noticed that Moses didn't have a team working with him. He was the judge of the Israelite, and people would come to him from sun up to sun down to seek redress. As a result, the whole process was slow and strenuous for both Moses and the people. Every single person with a case in court had to go through him. This was an impossible situation.

Do you know what this would mean? First, consider that the Israelites numbered over two million. This meant some people never got to have their cases heard or settled. Also, it means they made little progress in their own lives because they spent the whole day waiting for their turns.

When Jethro saw this, he immediately called Moses aside and rebuked him. He told him that his leadership style would endanger him and his people. He needed an upgrade. He advised him to build a team of judges. Some were to oversee thousands, hundreds, twenties and so on, this way, things would be done faster and with more efficiency. Success will be achieved when a team is involved.

Moses' mistake was that he neglected teamwork and carried unnecessary burden. It's possible that he felt he was the most knowledgeable person for the job. After all, he was passing judgment according to God's laws that was handed to him personally by God. But Moses was able to discover the value for teamwork and put it to good use.

Have you been like Moses? Are you carrying that burden all alone? Think about the people you are hurting because you want to do it all alone. I urge you to allow this lesson to speak to you as Jethro spoke to Moses. The Bible calls Moses the meekest man who ever lived; His leadership style wasn't the best, but he learned and became a great leader. Learn from Moses today on the value of teamwork.

PETER: A MAN WHO WAS ALWAYS TEAM MINDED

Another biblical example we can learn from is Peter. Peter was a knowledgeable leader. Of all Jesus's disciples, he worked closest to the Master. He knew his Master's business intricately. Yet he always saw the need for teamwork.

He was a leader that understood the peculiarities of his team members and was ready to put them to good use. Even while Jesus was on earth, Peter was able to discern that John the beloved was the closest to Jesus. This didn't spark jealousy in Peter. Instead, he used it as a strategy.

When Jesus said one of His disciples will betray Him, Peter wanted to know who Jesus spoke about. But He knew that for His Master to speak in parables, this information wasn't for everyone. So it would take someone who Jesus had a highly intimate relationship with to access such a secret. Therefore, Peter asked John the beloved to probe Jesus for more Intel, which he did.

After Jesus' death, Peter was such a team-minded that he noticed the vacancy amongst the apostles. He was the one who insisted, according to God's will, that another person ought to take Judas Iscariot's position as an Apostle. He could have dismissed the need, probably on the basis that 11 apostles were enough. But He knew the value of every team member, alongside wanting to do God's will.

It was under his leadership that the deacons were chosen to become a part of the church's leadership team. During this period, the early church flourished and increased. They had a culture of selling their properties to meet the needs of every member. And they also took care of widows.

However, because the apostles were limited, the widows of the Grecian Jews were neglected in the daily distribution of food, and this caused murmuring. But the twelve apostles under the leadership of Peter solved the problem quickly. Their answer to this dilemma was to increase their team size by selecting seven deacons for the job.

They explained that their work wasn't to serve tables but to give attention to prayer and the ministry of the word. They then had to delegate this other task to their new teammates. This action shows how much the apostles valued teamwork; it reflects the team-mindedness of their leader, Peter.

They knew their true success didn't come from trying to do everything by themselves. The Apostles had an all-hands-on-deck mentality.

Are you team-minded? Do you see your team as a solution? The early church grew, and the apostles knew they needed extra hands and brains. This shows that a leader who isn't team-minded will remain small. For the sake of your vision, learn from Peter. Become team-minded!

JESUS: HE CAME, CALLED AND COMMISSIONED

What about our ultimate leader – Jesus Christ. We've so much learned from His life and leadership pattern. But what lessons can we learn from Him about teamwork?

Jesus is God revealed in the flesh. We established earlier that God's nature is teamwork, and we see Jesus expressing this truth. While on earth, Jesus, although he was God in every way, chose to do everything He did through teamwork. In fact, His life revealed that vision is not for an individual, it is for a team. Here are some lessons to learn from Jesus:

❖ **Jesus prayed for His team** – He knew the value of a team in fulfilling a vision. For this reason, he didn't select his apostles casually. He chose His team prayerfully. A team is only as strong as its weakest link, so he knew that the kind of persons He recruited was vital to His success as a leader. Luke 6:12-13 says, *"One day soon afterward, Jesus went up on a mountain to pray, and he prayed to God all night. At daybreak, he called together all of his disciples and chose twelve of them to be apostles..."*

Jesus stayed up all night praying because he knew that for His mission to be a success, he needed to get the right team. every person He was going to work with had to be in sync with His assignment.

How much do you value teamwork? Are you careful in selecting people to join your team?

❖ **Jesus empowered His team** – There's no other leader like Jesus. While some leaders would want to outshine the team and be the best, Jesus wanted His team to be the best. Consequently, He empowered them. Jesus was a miracle worker. It was part of His mission. But He didn't want to be the only effective person on the team. He desired that His disciples were just like Him. In Matthew 10:1, Jesus empowered His team, *"And when he had called unto him his twelve disciples, he gave them power against unclean spirits, to cast them out, and to heal all manner of sickness and all manner of disease."*

Valuing teamwork also includes ensuring that every member of your team improves. Empowering your team can mean that you train them, help them improve and unleash their potential.

❖ **Jesus commissioned His team** – Jesus didn't just pray for His team or empower them. He commissioned them. He gave them instructions, conferred some form of responsibility and authority on them. Jesus didn't need to give His disciples a strategy for winning. They were His winning strategy.

The Bible reveals that Jesus gave them instructions to go to the same places He intended to go. He gave them opportunities to grow and own the vision. Luke 10:1 (KJV) says, "*After these things the Lord appointed other seventy also, and sent them two and two before his face into every city and place, whither he himself would come.*" Jesus sent out 70 people to do exactly what He did. Later on, after His death, He did the same thing, but with a larger crowd.

You can say that apart from dying for humanity, Jesus' greatest strategy for redemption is getting a team. In Mark 16, Jesus commissions His disciples to go into the world and preach the gospel. Their assignment was to create other teams. Think about it. A vision that recruits others to pursue it.

Do you allow your teammates to do some actual work? Have you given each member opportunities to realize their potentials? Learn from Jesus and commission your team. Through the commission, Jesus told His disciples that His vision was the whole world. Teamwork will expand your vision.

❖ **Jesus valued the ideas of His team members** – if you study Jesus' relationship with His disciples, you'll notice that they felt free to say anything around Him. They aired their own opinions as frequently as possible. They asked questions and made the most outrageous demands. All these go to show how much Jesus valued teamwork. Friend, you can't value teamwork without valuing others' opinions and ideas.

In John chapter 6, where Jesus fed the five thousand miraculously, Jesus listened to His team. He didn't just start acting on the idea he had. He was concerned about the crowd. They had been with Him for three days and He wanted to feed them.

So He asked Philip, "*Whence shall we buy bread that these may eat?*" in verse 6, the Bible reveals that Jesus knew what to do but was just testing Philip. It was all part of His training program.

Every leader ought to take a leaf from Jesus' book. Who knows how many times He asked His teammates for their own opinions. By so doing, He trained them as well as showed them their value. Jesus sincerely desired that His disciples have success-oriented ideas.

If you want to be a great leader, you have to value other people's ideas.

CHECKLIST FOR AN EFFECTIVE TEAMWORK

I know by now you have increased your value for teamwork. I know you really want to create your team or move forward to achieve greatness with your team if you already have one. But how can you be sure that you have effective teamwork? I want to let you in on the fundamentals of effective collaboration. I want you to think about each one of them as they relate to your team.

1. Clear purpose, vision, mission and game plan:

Without the knowledge of the purpose of a thing, they say, abuse is inevitable. The truth is people will not follow you when they do not know where you are taking them. So, have you identified the purpose of your team? Does everyone know why the group was created? Where are you going? What do you need to get there?

2. Clear roles and responsibilities

Roles and responsibilities must be defined and accepted as performance indicators among your team members. A performing team must have measurable outputs or results that express the level of efficiency of every member of the group. As a team leader, what are your expectations for your organization? What do you want each team member to achieve? What have you decided to accomplish based on each person's contribution?

3. Don't neglect a measure of Informality

The next is to consider and assess the level of ease of collaboration in your team. Do team members feel comfortable with each other?

Are they able to sit together without tension and stress? How easily do they get things done with and through one another?

4. Access the level of participation among team members

It's time to start assessing the level of participation of each member of the team. Do they have a role and daily involvement with the team? How eager are they to engage or collaborate on a given task?

One effective way to monitor and measure participation is active listening and eagerness to ask relevant questions. That is, your team members want to know what the other person is thinking, and they are free to speak their mind in a friendly atmosphere.

Likewise, they allow civilized (polite and friendly) disagreement and feel comfortable disagreeing with one another.

5. How do you reach consensus decisions?

Here, you need to assess the way and manner by which your team makes important decisions. Do they select the best approach to issues? Or do they find it hard to conclude and decide over an issue?

6. How open is your communication?

Are they able to express their opinion? Do they keep secrets or valuable information from each other? Are there ulterior motives among team members?

FINALLY...

"Two are better than one because they have a good return for their labor:

If either of them falls down, one can help the other up. But pity anyone who falls and has no one to help him up.

Also, if two lie down together, they will keep warm. But how can one keep warm alone?

Though one may be overpowered, two can defend themselves. A cord of three strands is not quickly broken."

-Ecclesiastes 4:9-12

How far do you want to go? How high do you want to climb? How much do you want to achieve? How quickly do you want to succeed? How easily do you want to excel? And how strong do you want to be?

THINKING BIG? YOUR ANSWER IS TEAMWORK!

LESSON 8

WILLINGNESS TO LEARN AND RECEIVE ADVICE

"A wise man will hear and will increase learning; and a man of understanding shall attain unto wise counsels."

-Proverbs 1:5

Seeking, as well as giving advice is vital to effective leadership and decision making. Many in leadership have the misconception that they are supposed to be all-knowing. That is, they believe as leaders, they should have answers to all questions and must be able to proffer solutions to all problems. But this is an impossible feat. You will always have areas of strengths and weaknesses. Therefore, every leader needs others to make their vision become a reality.

Due to this error in belief, only few leaders seek advice. They see it as a sign of weakness and incompetence. As a result, they put their team and vision in jeopardy. Since they are trying to save their face, they refuse to seek help when they need it the most.

Think about this for a moment: Can a leader shoulder the great responsibility of decision making alone? Have you noticed that advisers surround leaders who take up important government positions? Why is this the case? Is it because they are clueless? Of course not!

If you want to build a house and you didn't study architecture, what do you do? Hire an expert, right? The house might be yours, and you know how you want it to look, but other people do the building. It's the same thing in leadership.

A leader's job is to drive the vision. They motivate and mobilize others to commit to it and make it a reality. Thus, a leader doesn't have to be the smartest. They just need to know how to utilize the skills and expertise of the people around them. This includes being willing to learn and receive advice. By so doing, they increase their chances of success and make better decisions.

Do you want to be a great leader? Then you have to understand the importance of listening to advisers. In truth, great leaders accept their limitations and are willing to accept relevant advice.

IT TAKES TWO TO TANGO, BUT IT TAKES A MULTITUDE TO LEAD

"Where there is no counsel, purposes are disappointed: but in the multitude of counsellors they are established."

Proverbs 15:22

Are you familiar with the popular adage, *We are the decisions we make?* What do you think it means? Well, I believe it means our life choices determine our results. What you did in the past affects your present, while the things you do in the present affect the future. Do you understand this?

Well, this principle also applies to leadership. Your success as a leader depends on your ability to make the right decisions. It was John C. Maxwell, who said, *"Everything rises and falls on leadership."* The actions and inactions of a business executive can either make the company's stocks rise or fall. Decision making is an invaluable aspect of leadership. Therefore, it's not a one-man's job.

As a matter of fact, the scripture above states that it takes a multitude of advisers to achieve success. Can you imagine that?! It also says that where there is no good advice, a purpose will fail.

No wonder some leaders have an alarming number of special advisers attached to them. For example, besides the official cabinet, the U.S President has about 18 senior advisers on his staff. Apart from these, he has a vast number of special advisers on virtually every subject of importance.

You might be wondering, why the fuss over a leader's decisions? Well, I'll have you remember that the President is also the commander-in-chief of the country's armed forces. He has the codes to America's nuclear warheads. And such a powerful leader would need to be objective and circumspect because his decisions won't only affect him, but billions of other people. So the more the advisers, the safer a leader's decisions.

For that reason, as a leader, you have to come to terms with your ignorance. The truth is, people in power can be excessively ego-centric. But it takes a good leader to put aside his ego and seek the counsel of others.

Don't you find it interesting that on the subject of teamwork, the Bible says that two are better than one? Yet when it comes to taking advice in leadership, the Bible recommends a multitude. Wow! So it takes two to tango, to work together in harmony, but it takes a multitude to lead.

Do you aspire for greatness as a leader? Then you can't compromise on having a listening ear. Indeed, great leaders can admit their limitations and seek advice.

I NEED ADVICE, BUT MY EGO SAYS, "SHUTUP".

Egotism is the anesthetic which nature gives us to deaden the pain of being a fool

Dr. Herbert Shofield

I'm sure you know human beings have a lot in common. However, I want to show you something we all have that makes us spit out advice like bad food. I bet you wonder, *what can this be?* It's an EGO: self-importance.

According to John C. Maxwell, "*Leaders who are overly concerned with self-promotion eventually wreck their legacies. And, in their efforts to exalt themselves, they often end up looking ridiculous*". The first step he offered in *Burying Your Ego* as a leader is to seek feedback. This means listening to and accepting other people's advice and opinion.

But the thing is, having an ego makes us want to protect our sense of self and identity. This makes us believe we always know what we are doing (even when we're in deep water), and that we can handle anything life throws at us on our own. This is because we want to give the idea of being in control; we want to be the captain of our destinies. And revealing that you don't know what to do, looks a lot like to *cry-uncle* (admitting defeat). No one wants to show weakness! As a result, it's more natural to reject advice than to take it.

YOUR PERSONALITY DETERMINES YOUR RESPONSE TO ADVICE

Now, it's common knowledge that no matter how one might feel, taking advice is a smart move, especially in critical situations or matters of life and death. This suggests that people have to develop the habit of seeking and implementing advice consciously.

Yet your personality determines your response to advice. Psychologists have discovered that concerning this subject, there are three kinds of people:

1. **People who reject advice spontaneously:** When they listen to you, it's not to understand, but to defend their own beliefs and actions. People in this category delude themselves that they are always right. Continue incorrigibly down the wrong path even when they fail repeated, they often say, *I know what I'm doing.*

2. **People who love the comfort zone**: Even if they value the advice someone gives them, they never put it to work. This is the category of the multitude. Do you find yourself among this crowd? These people are creative; they can come up with a million excuses for not putting a piece of advice to good use.

    One bible character that exemplifies this kind of personality is the rich ruler in Luke chapter 18. This successful man came to Jesus, desiring the key to inheriting eternal life. He passed all the qualifications except one. He kept the Law of Moses to the letter. He must have studied Jesus from far and also followed His teachings. He probably heard all Jesus had been teaching and had weighed them with his life. Yet, he felt something was still missing, so he ran after Jesus, seeking advice on the issue of eternal life.

Without hesitation, Jesus told him what to do, and the man immediately replied that he had kept the law from his youth. Consequently, Jesus looked at him with love and gave him one last advice, which is, *"sell all that you have and distribute it to the poor, and you will have treasure in heaven. Then come, follow me"*. This was the opportunity of a lifetime for this ruler. He had finally received the advice that he sought. But how did he respond?

The Bible says that when he heard Jesus' advice, he became sad. What was requested of him was too great a price to pay. He knew it was good advice, but he couldn't put it to good use. He loved his riches. It is his comfort zone.

Are you like this fellow? What have you done with all the million-dollar suggestions you've been receiving. Wouldn't your business be better if you had taken that advice? Obviously, you need to change your response today.

3. **These people are endangered species:** They are those who listen carefully when advice is given. They critically analyze it, ensuring its wisdom and relevance to their situation. When they hear good advice, they embrace it like a mother cuddling her child. These people actually implement advice if they find it helpful.

In the Bible, someone who had this kind of personality was Moses. When his Father-in-law gave him leadership advice, he weighed it for relevance, he saw it was a perfect fit for his current situation, and he gladly embraced it. What was the outcome of this? A more efficient and successful leadership.

What category do you fit into? How do you respond to advice? Are you the kind that never does anything with good advice? Well, no matter the category you find yourself, there's room for improvement. Great leaders seek and take good advice, and you can become one today.

THREE INTERESTING REASONS YOU PROBABLY WON'T SEEK OR TAKE ADVICE

Sun Tzu, in his book *The Art of War,* made a profound statement, he said, *"If you know the enemy and know yourself, you need not fear the results of a hundred battles."* This implies that success comes from knowing what hinders you from your goal; including your personal limitations. It was the Apostle, Paul, who said to his spiritual son Timothy, *"Take heed to yourself."* This was part of his advice to him on things that would help him succeed.

So, in the light of this, let's look at three reasons why you probably won't seek or take advice:

1. **A difference in perception** – One reason why you probably won't take advice is that people see things differently. The way you perceive your situation will differ from how others might see it. This means that sometimes you might be oblivious to your missteps. Yet it's crystal clear to everyone that you're doomed to fail.

   Such a thing is possible as those on the outside have an unbiased view of the situation. Since they are uninvolved, they can see things more clearly. But you can't. The reason is, you are too wrapped up in your situation and life. As a result, you're likely to reject whatever advice they give you.

   A biblical example of this is Job. He was going through a period of trial in his life. He had lost all his wealth, and his children were killed in a natural disaster. All these things happened in a day. This great evil that befell Job caused him to mourn for days and put on sackcloth.

   When his friends came to visit him, they were dumbfounded by his misfortune. Greatly sympathizing with him, they mourned with him for several days before uttering a word. Finally, they spoke their minds and offered advice.

However, Job couldn't accept their advice because of their different perceptions. When they found him devastated, they saw a man who God was punishing for his sins. While he saw himself as a righteous man, being punished for a crime he didn't commit. Due to their conflicting views, their advice was not relevant to Job.

If someone advices you from a different point of view, don't immediately reject it, instead, examine it for relevance. Try to see it from their perspective. You need to appraise what you're going through objectively. Attempt to perceive the situation from different angles. I believe these will make you more open to seeking and receiving advice.

2. **Fear of the unknown** – When it comes to fear of the unknown, everyone is guilty as charged. How many times has spine-chilling fear bullied you out of success? Can you recount how many business opportunities you've ignored because of fear?

However, it's not all fear. It's also a love for the comfort zone. The reason is, what is familiar to us is safe and tolerable. But the unknown, even when it's a promotion, looks downright dangerous.

The fear of the unknown is probably one of the reasons you don't take advice. Most times, we need to take new and bold steps to make progress; good advice will motivate you to do so. But often, we get terrified of the outcome. We think, *what if it doesn't work out as planned? What kind of changes will this move bring?*

Have you been here, friend? Do you remember having to make the choice of sticking to the status quo or take that leap into new territory? Has a fear of the unknown disabled your progress? Possibly you end up hoping that things will figure themselves out, even when you know it all depends on your decision.

You have to realize that things don't work, people do. It all depends on your ability to embrace good advice when you see it. Do so now and create the success you desire.

3. **A careless approach to life** – Do you take responsibility for your successes and failures? People who tend to play the blame game will find it hard to change their ways. Thus, making listening to advice difficult.

If you're living in denial and refusing to accept that you are wrong, you can't improve. You don't want to be this kind of person for you'll find yourself repeating cycles you should have outgrown.

It also means that you will believe you are right and that your actions have nothing to do with your outcome. Hence, you won't seek advice or value it. A careless approach to life indicates a person doesn't live deliberately and always counts on luck.

Nevertheless, if you find yourself here, there's no need for self-pity or condemnation. What you have to do is to change your perspective. Develop a more intentional approach to life and take responsibility for results. This will have a renewing effect on your mind. Before you know it, you'll begin to detect where the problems in your life, team, or business come from. And this will prompt you to seek and take the relevant advice that will make you successful.

FIVE AMAZING REASONS YOU SHOULD LISTEN TO ADVICE

1. **Right information can determine your success** – When people have conversations, they tend to speak from their wealth of knowledge and experience. Sometimes, what a person says in one sentence took them ten years to discover. Someone once said: *"If I have ever seen further, it's because I climbed the shoulders of those that are ahead of me."* Perhaps, the key to your success can be handed to you over dinner at a restaurant.

The Bible says in Matthew 7:8 that all those who seek a thing, eventually find what they were searching for. As a leader in your field, listening to advice is one of the best ways to get new ideas and innovations.

Why do people attend business seminars and conferences? What's the motive behind reading self-help books or the biographies of great men and women? People are in search of information that gives them what they are looking for. For some, it's fulfillment, while for others, its fame, and for most, it is success.

2. **The duty of leadership** - Being a good leader requires listening and considering all the options. Part of your job is to give everyone a chance to present their ideas. This is relevant to all fields. It doesn't matter if you're a businessman or a doctor.

As an employer, you have to remember that everyone has the right to speak without being discriminated or ignored. Indeed, listening to people's advice and valuing their ideas is characteristic of a good leader. It will increase your influence and chances of success. Consequently, those around you will know that you truly value them, thereby, support your vision.

Also, as a leader, you have the important duty of making decisions that affect the livelihood, future, and even the health of others. The truth is, nobody is smart or knowledgeable enough to handle such great responsibility alone.

3. **Other people's ideas might be better than yours** – A leader who is serious about success won't care about who gets the credit. Rather they will be focused on producing results. Such a leader will be open to other people's ideas.

There's a popular saying that *Ideas rule the world*. Friend, this is not an exaggeration. Every invention we see in the world today was the figment of someone's imagination. It was an idea. Think of the amazing discoveries in medicine on the cure for deadly diseases. And how about the intelligent strategies that are developed by the staff of companies all over the world?

Ideas are important for the creation of new jobs and opportunities. It is needed most frequently for problem-solving.

Certainly, one person cannot monopolize all the fantastic ideas in the world. While you might be clueless about how to solve a problem, a colleague or teammate might have a million ideas at hand.

Yes, your ideas are good, but other people's ideas might be better. True leaders aren't interested in projecting themselves; their interests are the success of the business and the improvement of their team. Thus, these kind of leaders give everybody an equal chance to express their ideas. And their mantra is: let the best idea win.

4. **To avoid conflicts** – As a leader, you have to make more allies than enemies. This means avoiding any behavior or action that produces conflict. Conflict in the workplace and unhealthy competition has disastrous effects on productivity. Why is this important?

Well, conflicts tend to ensue when people's ideas and opinions are taken for granted. They feel trampled on, frustration sets in, this is bad for business. Such skirmishes are rampant in politics and organizations.

A great leader is careful to win allies diplomatically. This doesn't mean allowing yourself to be influenced or taking wrong counsel, No. However, a leader should be able to make his colleagues or teammates feel valued, no matter the kind of suggestions they make.

Don't reject any person's idea outright. Make sure they know that you considered their advice. Even if you decide you want to do something different, be intelligent about it. You can say something like, *I considered what you said, but I want us to try this out first*, or *That was a good suggestion, but how about we work with this instead.*

Acceptance doesn't mean implementation. When you show people that you value their opinions, the workplace becomes a peaceful environment, a place where success is possible.

5. **It will improve your staff or teammates** – Do you know that listening to people can improve their abilities and develop their potentials? It seems farfetched, right? Nonetheless, this is a fact.

You're a trainer as a leader. Your team will only be efficient when you give them opportunities to improve. If you're a teacher, you'll agree with me that the best students are those whose opinions and ideas are valued. A teacher who allows students to share their views on subjects openly is indirectly developing their potentials.

Reason being that, when people get a chance to see the outcome of their ideas or opinions, they are challenged and inspired to become better. Success produces self-confidence and a desire to achieve more, while failure is seen as a challenge.

The more people see the results of their ideas, the more they are inspired to improve. Important lessons can be learned from failure. And people have more faith when they succeed.

Hence, by listening to people and taking their advice, you're giving them opportunities to learn and grow. In the long run, their development will contribute to the success of your vision.

FIVE STEPS TO KNOWING WHAT ADVICE TO RUN WITH

Undoubtedly, good advice is an excellent tool for building any structure. Whether it's a company, a business, a team, or a relationship, the right advice can work wonders. However, you have to develop your discerning skills. You must have the ability to know what advice to run with.

You know the popular saying, *Rome wasn't built in a day*. It means that great things take time and effort. So you need to be extra careful about the kind of advice you receive. Wrong advice is like the atomic bomb; it can turn your *Rome* into *Hiroshima*. Let's take a look at five steps to knowing what advice to run with:

1. **Be aware of context** – The first step is to be conscious of context. In other words, the events surrounding an occurrence.

It's like the background story or the buildup. You have to keep in mind that good advice can be gotten anywhere, most times, from the most unexpected sources.

However, to know which advice to run with, you need to be aware of the context in which it is given. Because most times, bad advice sounds good. Knowing the context of an advice entails predicting outcomes. Ask yourself, *Is this advice going to produce the desired result? Does it provide the needed solution?* Be sure it's to your advantage.

This also refers to the situation leading to the moment when the advice is given and the circumstances surrounding it. For example, it will be unwise to take advice on how to improve your business from people you're currently competing with. What about advice from someone who has been drinking?

Do you want to be open to good ideas but minimize mistakes? Then context is vital.

2. **Check the motive** – This step is important in fishing out toxic advice. The next time you're given a piece of advice, ask yourself, *why is this person instructing me to do so and so?. What do they stand to gain? Is this person truly concerned? Do they have an ulterior motive?* Always try to read in-between the lines to know people's intentions.

Funny enough, it's best to take advice from someone who has something to lose or gain. The reason is if they're affected by the outcome, their advice would be objective and candid. Now, I don't mean people who want to deceive you. No, I'm referring to investors and probable business partners. Someone once said, *"Don't base your decisions on the advice of people who don't have to live with the result."*

Jesus is the perfect example of a great leader. He had great value for other people's ideas and opinions. But He also valued motive. In John chapter 2, Jesus performed many miracles that caused the people who saw him to admire him greatly.

A lot of them expressed their belief in Him as the Messiah, but Jesus refused to value what they said. He didn't make Himself vulnerable to them. The Bible says it was because He knew what was in them. He knew what was in their hearts (he understood their motives).

Your ability to check for motives the next time you are advised might save you your job, or preserve your business.

3. **Guard against unsolicited advice** – Unsolicited advice is the most common form of advice. It's the kind that you didn't ask for. It is to you what a weed is to a farmer- UNWANTED. In truth, most people just want to be heard. What they say to you doesn't stem from genuine concern for your success. These kind of people give advice that lacks real substance. They can sell you tell tales and fantasies that'll make wonderland look real, all in a bid to attract attention to themselves.

Can you remember when Jesus rebuked Peter, one of His most trusted disciples? It was because of unsolicited advice. You'll agree with me that the desire to attract attention through tell tales and exaggerated stories, is an evil one. So, Jesus was spot-on when He said to Peter, *"Get thee behind me, Satan."* Jesus wasn't calling Peter Satan, rather, He was addressing the evil desire that had prompted the advice.

Even as you aspire to become a better leader by listening to others, you have to watch out for cheap suggestions. They are disasters waiting to happen.

4. **Verify the source** – Some people love to appear knowledgeable. This prompts them to offer their opinion on every subject under discussion. They peddle rumors and dish out information without ascertaining its authenticity. The next time you're

listening to advice, verify the source. Is it an assumption? Can it be a new, untested idea? Or is it a reliable information?

It'll help to ask your informant for the source of his statistics skillfully. The source should determine if it goes into the trash or goes home in your pocket.

Do you know that during His earthly ministry, Jesus only valued information after He had verified the source? Matthew chapter 16, brings us to an interesting scene set in Caesarea Philippi. Here Jesus asked His disciples, *"Who do men say that I am?"* His disciples had heard a lot of rumors and speculations, so they were armed with information. They replied eagerly, *"Some say you are John the Baptist, others say you are Elijah, and others still, Jeremiah or one of the Prophets."*

Well, Jesus didn't place much value on rumors and assumptions, so He asked the men who had been working closely with Him: *"who do you say I am?"*

These men knew Jesus. Their answer had to be an informed one, not an assumption. In spite of this, only Peter had the confidence to speak up. He said, *"You are the Messiah, the Son of the living God."* What a revelation! This was an answer that Jesus could accept, and he expressed His delight. He knew the source of this information. It was from God Himself, so He valued it.

Have you lost something precious to you because you didn't verify the source of information? The information or advice you run with as a leader is important. It can help you build or destroy what's already standing. No matter the mistakes you've made in the past, you can make amends by learning from Jesus.

5. **Look out for experience and expertise** – Would you like to get a drug prescription from a farmer? What about dropping off your car at the carpenter's shop for repairs? I bet your answer is No. Why? The answer is simple: Expertise. In both cases, they were unsuitable for the job.

The last step we'll consider in knowing the right advice to take, has a lot to do with the proficiency of your informant. Always ensure that the person giving you advice is either experienced in that subject or is an expert. This will prevent unnecessary regrets and losses.

Many top company executives and business owners have made decisions that cost them millions of dollars. Their error wasn't a lack of advisers; they failed because the people they listened to were either not experts in the field of interest or had no real-life experience.

FINALLY...

Your ability to accept your limitations and take good advice as a leader reflects strength. According to Proverbs, seeking counsel and learning is a sign of wisdom, not weakness. Concerning this, Andrew Carnegie said, *"It marks a big step in your development when you come to realize that other people can help you do a better job than you can do alone."*

Jesus, who is the perfect leadership example, made a profound statement. He said in John 5:30 (NIV), *"By myself, I can do nothing: I judge only as I hear, and my judgment is just, for I seek not to please myself but Him who sent me."* Here Jesus was expressing the fact that He didn't work alone. Everything Jesus did was in response to what the Father advised and instructed. He never acted alone. Jesus also said he was all about pleasing the Father; His priority was making sure God's vision was a success.

What an incredible example we have? Some people who aren't even equal with God like Jesus was, believed they could succeed on their own. Take a look at what King Nebuchadnezzar said in Daniel 4:30, *"he said, 'Is not this the great Babylon I have built as the royal residence, by my mighty power and for the glory of my majesty?'"*

Do you see the difference between Jesus' statement and that of the heathen King? Jesus confessed His dependence on God. He couldn't achieve success alone. But Nebuchadnezzar claimed all the glory. He didn't recognize God or his servant, who served him loyally.

So how did Jesus end up? He succeeded in fulfilling His vision, today, He remains the most influential leader in existence; He is the head of the church. On the other hand, Nebuchadnezzar's arrogance and pride led to his fall. God stripped him of his glory and for seven years, he ate grasses like an animal.

Surely, the road to success is not for those who don't take good advice. It is for those who like Jesus, would say, *"Of myself, I can do nothing."* Great leaders are those, who accept their limitations and can take good advice.

LESSON 9

THE VALUE OF TIME

"The way we spend our time defines who we are."

-Jonathan Estrin

D r. Myles Munroe once said, "Every human being is given the same amount of time. What you become in life is determined by how you use your 24 hours." What a profound and true statement.

Have you noticed that you don't look like anybody? Neither do you talk nor walk like anybody else. In fact, your hands are not like anybody's. Your fingerprint is unique to you, and everybody is unique in their own right.

Nevertheless, there's only one thing that every human being has in common, that is TIME. It's the reason why we talk about stress or being busy; we're all trying to keep up with it. It tends to be like God; it respects nobody. However, it will surprise you that time is the reason we are all different in terms of our achievements and social standing.

Have you ever wondered why some people are so smart? Or why that lady in your neighborhood is so successful? Or probably why a role model is so influential and on top of their game? What about the employee that keeps getting better at his job?

Well, the simple answer is - TIME. We are all gifted with the same 24 hours daily, but we use our time differently. Some invest their time doing meaningful things that improve their lives and others'. While others spend or waste their time on irrelevant activities. What you invest your time on, determines your results and outcomes.

In other words, time gives us the same opportunity but the way we use our time makes the difference. As a matter of fact, every variation in society is as a result of time. For instance, the gap between the rich and the poor, the successful and unsuccessful, the smart kid, and the dullard, is time. What does each person do with their time? How do you use your time? Are you investing your time on books that'll make you successful? Or are you the type that spends a lot of your time on frivolities?

Also, I believe that time is the setting God put into life to enable us to explore our uniqueness. If what you're becoming depends on how you use your time, then you have the power to customize your life to produce only success.

A great part of a leader's time is public property. There's just so much to do and too many people to attend to. Only a leader has an in-depth understanding of the expression: time flies. If there was a superpower all leaders crave, it would be the ability to control time. Although, you can't pause time like music, it can be managed; it is this ability that makes you a great leader.

Consequently, as a leader, you have to value, understand and harness time as a tool to achieve your goals and fulfill purpose wherever you find yourself. Those who are significant in life happen to be more deliberate and strict about the use of their time. Since they are about investing and not spending time, every minute becomes an opportunity to make tremendous profits and returns.

Thus, if you want to be a great leader, you must be someone who values time and maximizes it in your pursuit of vision; as one who charts the course for others.

UNDERSTANDING THE GIFT OF TIME

Time is a gift from God. It marks new beginning and is a source of hope. People can remain steadfast in their trials because they know it won't last long. Try to recall the worst thing you've ever experienced and imagine continuously reliving it over and over again. Won't that be horrible? Thank God for time.

Sincerely, I believe time is God's gift to humanity. Also, we react to time the same way we respond to a present or gift.

For instance, imagine you had an appointment with a top client. On your way to the meeting, you got held up in traffic and you couldn't make it in time. Supposing this appointment was of great importance to the next phase of your business or organization. You'd be sad and frustrated, right? However, imagine you called the client and he or she listened to you calmly and agreed to meet with you some other time, how would you feel?

Let me guess: happy, excited, grateful, or gracious? Well, this is the same way you would feel if you got a gift.

The Cambridge English Dictionary defines time as the part of existence that is measured in minutes, days, years, etc...or this process considered as a whole. In physics, time is defined in terms of it's measurement: it is what a clock reads.

Dr. Myles Munroe said: "We measure life in terms of TIME; we define life by TIME because life is determined by what we do with TIME. Life is qualified by TIME; life is also the passing of TIME. Life is also stopped by TIME when you die; TIME stops. When you die, you move out of time into what we call eternity. Time is temporary, but life is eternal."

Because time is a gift from God, we must show gratitude to Him by using our time wisely as faithful stewards of this precious gift. Since time is life, we must not squander or waste other people's time. We must be grateful for it and gracious because of it. As a leader, you want people to be able to trust you with their time.

HOW TO MANAGE YOUR TIME

Successful people have time management skills and strategies that help to achieve critical tasks that add meaning to their lives. If you have to choose between success and failure. What will it be? Do you opt for the pain of discipline or that of regret? Here are some keys that will help to manage your time:

1. **Be organized** – Time management is key to maximizing your life and becoming a success. To manage your time correctly, you have to manage yourself first. Are you a disorganized person? Do you drop things where they shouldn't be, then spend the whole day looking for them? Do you forget your appointments? Or maybe you wake up in the morning without knowing what you want to achieve at the end of the day?

   Most average people are guilty of all the above. But if you want to be a great leader, you must learn how to lead and govern yourself.

   First of all, it'll help if you had a daily routine. You need to cram the numerous tasks and activities that make up your day into a regular cycle and avoid breaking it.

   Second, have a to-do list that shows in detail, all your activities for the day. For this, you can use sticky-notes, a journal, or a notice board. Most times, the tricky thing is not having a to-do-list but sticking to it. But you'll have to discipline yourself to get the desired results.

   Third, arrange your home and workspace. Everything must be in its right position to avoid spending more of your time searching for things, avoid clutter by reorganizing your clothes, files, documents and personal effects regularly.

2. **Set goals** – How successful will a leader be without a vision? Well, such a person's chances are slim. And this also applies to your personal and corporate life. Remember, you're trying to lead yourself more effectively to manage your time better.

   Therefore, you need to set goals. Write out both long-term and short-term goals: what do you want to achieve in a day, week, month, year, decade, etc. For example, if you desire to improve your knowledge in business, you can set a reading goal by deciding to read two books on marketing every month.

3. **Prioritize** – Setting priorities will enable you maximize your time. It entails focusing your energy on what is most important at a

particular time. Brain Tracy came up with the perfect strategy for prioritizing called the ABCDE Method.

In this formula, the letter A represents tasks that are of utmost importance. Failure to do them has dire consequences: losing a client or getting fired. While B tasks are those that have lesser effects, for example, a pizza delivery guy might deliver his goods to a client behind schedule and get nothing but a complaint.

Then, the letter C Stands for tasks that are necessary but have no consequences: your life would be excellent, with or without them. The letter D represents a job that can be delegated. One rule in prioritizing is to allot every task that falls into this category to someone else, thus, creating more time for the A tasks.

Finally, E stands for eliminate. These tasks fall into the category of things that are no longer necessary. As a result, you need to remove them from your to-do list.

An example of leaders who knew the importance of prioritization in the bible were the Twelve Apostles. These men were the leaders of the early church, an organized organism that continued to grow immensely.

At this time, they had a system for meeting the needs of every believer; they sold their properties and brought the money to the church. Over time, the number of disciples increased so much that the leaders were unaware some persons were neglected.

Soon, there was a complaint that the Grecian widows were not given their daily rations. Immediately, the apostles assembled the people to solve the problem. They told the people they couldn't leave their A task to attend to a D task.

Their priority was to give themselves to prayer and the ministry of the word. As a result, they delegated the duty of administering the daily portions of food and clothing to seven chosen men.

Therefore, as a leader, concentrate on the A tasks: prioritize.

4. **Live in the moment** – This means focusing on where you are per time. Most people never live in the moment and this makes them less productive.

While they're at the breakfast table, they are already thinking of their job. Meanwhile, at work, their mind is on their spouse or kids. Such people never concentrate on the task at hand. Thus they don't live a full life; they are always stressed and anxious. Concerning this, Jim Rohn said, "Wherever you are, be there. Lifestyle is not something we do; it is something we experience. And until we learn to be there, we will never master the art of living well."

The key is to focus on what you're doing with all your mind and strength; such that, once you close from the office, you can retire for the day. This way, both your corporate and private life will receive ample amounts of your time.

5. **Communicate effectively** – As a leader, maintaining effective communication in the workplace should be a priority. Failure to do so will cause unnecessary time-waste. Just imagine if an employee misunderstood your instructions. Or better still, you delegated a job to a teammate who didn't quite understand what was required. This would reduce productivity, use up time allotted to other tasks and might even cause losses.

Always ensure that your colleagues, employees, or teammates understand your instructions and directives. In addition, you also need to communicate efficiently with clients concerning appointments and meetings to save time. Form the habit of following up clients or business partners to confirm their availability for appointments or to reschedule if the need arises.

6. **Manage your stress** – There can't be any hard work without stress; it's a normal part of everyday life. Stress is not only negative. In fact, it may surprise you to know that there's good and bad stress.

The former is our natural reaction to things. We get excited, nervous, a thrill runs down our spine, etc.; research reveals that even the occurrence of something positive can produce stress. But the negative kind occurs when you perpetually struggle to meet up deadlines, and you're burdened with too much work.

Since you can't escape stress, what you need to do is manage it. You can do this by avoiding procrastination; it is the thief of time, and you don't want to carry over today's work to tomorrow. Secondly, focus on your strengths. You're not expected to be good at everything. Concentrating on the areas of your weakness will only slow down your productivity.

7. **Delegation** - If you're not going to focus on your weakness, what would happen to the other tasks? The answer is delegation. Always delegate tasks you know you're not good at to maximize your time and energy.

You also need to know the kind of tasks you don't want to delegate. Always handle high priority tasks yourself or entrust them to someone with some experience or expertise. The tasks you need to transfer to someone else are those with low or no consequence, just in case things go south.

BENEFITS OF MANAGING TIME

"Time is the currency of life."

Dr. Myles Munroe

Managing your time and investing in the right activity is like capitalizing money; you'll get fantastic returns on your investment. Honestly, when you manage your time effectively, there are benefits you get. Imagine being able to go to the mall and buy whatever you want. That would be the benefit of having enough money, wouldn't it? Also, maximizing and managing your time produces specific results.

Some of the benefits of managing time are,

1. **Increase in productivity and efficiency** – When you're able to manage your time more effectively, you'll discover that your work becomes more productive and efficient. As a leader, you have the duty of ensuring that your employees also manage their time. Through skills like goal setting, prioritization, delegation and much more, you can create the right atmosphere for competence and excellence.

2. **A reliable, professional reputation** – Time management is essential for maintaining a high level of quality and providing value for your clients. Most businesses and organizations miss deadlines and are unable to sustain the standard or class they are known for. This gives such firms, bad reputation. But time management will help you deliver on time and increase the quality of your product at a steady pace.

3. **Less stress** – There is no efficient management of time that doesn't include dealing with procrastination and focusing on priorities. This would ensure that you don't accumulate tasks and jobs are done at the right time. As a result, there will be a reduction in stress levels: for you and your organization at large.

4. **Increase in advancement opportunities** – One crucial benefit of managing time is the maximization of opportunities. Let's say you were able to finish contracts and deliver them on time, the client will be encouraged to entrust you with more work. Also, delegating tasks can increase the capacity of your firm to handle more work.

5. **Achievement of life and career goals** – Goal setting will help you achieve short term life and career goals while leading others. Without being deliberate about how you spend your time, you might become occupied with activities and still have little results.

CONSEQUENCES OF MISMANAGING TIME

"Time is what we want most, but what we use worst."

William Penn

There's one truth about time none of us can deny. No matter how good you are, you've once been bad at managing your time. Or perhaps you still are. If adequate and efficient use of your time brings about success, certainly, the abuse of it will produce failure. The consequences of time management can destroy your leadership or put you out of business. I call them the different shades of failure, some of them are:

1. **Missed deadlines** – Inadequate use of time has serious consequences. When you don't set goals or priorities, you might end up doing the most crucial work last. This would cause you to miss deadlines and have late deliveries. Your inability to handle procrastination can put you in a binder and make you stall on a job: carrying work over for months.

2. **Inefficient workflow** – A workflow simply means a group of people that a job needs to pass through to be complete. Whenever data goes through a system, a workflow has been established. But what if somebody relevant to a workflow didn't do his or her part because of poor time management? What happens? They disrupt the workflow, and this will lead to low productivity.

Most factory and industry jobs require workflow. If you're on a team, you can't achieve anything without the proper flow of data from one person to another. Every person must get the data they need at the right time; it's like passing the baton at a relay race.

3. **Poor work quality** – Mismanagement of time produces stress, which, in turn, brings about poor performance. Most employees and CEO's have to work late nights when they don't maximize their time correctly. Besides stress, doing a job

under pressure affects the quality of the work done; you won't be deliberate and meticulous as always.

4. **A poor reputation** – Mismanagement of time can make you cancel meetings frequently, repeatedly miss deadlines, decrease the quality of your work and so on. This can cause clients to begin to see you as untrustworthy and unreliable, which is terrible for your reputation. Mind you, many careers have been destroyed because of critics and bad reviews.

5. **Higher stress levels** – A clear sign of poor time management is when you have to do everything by yourself. This can put you under undue pressure. We saw earlier that delegation is a time management skill. Leaders who don't trust their employees or teammates to carry out essential tasks end up frustrated and stressed out. Effective delegation will reduce stress for everyone and will help you maximize time. Stress kills productivity and efficiency; it can ruin the quality of your work and stagnate your business. Avoid it.

TRUE LEADERS UTILIZE TIME

"...the sons of Issachar who had understanding of the times, to know what Israel ought to do..."

1Chronicles 12:32(NKJV)

Earlier, we discussed time as a gift from God. I believe it is God's will for us to use this gift and not be used by it. Most times, we end up getting ruled and controlled by time due to poor time management. Yet, God's desire is for you to master time, utilizing it to achieve your purpose and attain resounding success.

Today, the world is enthralled with the idea of time travel: being able to manipulate time. Presently scientists are trying to create the perfect time machine. The possibility of being able to travel back in time and correct mistakes is the dream of several people around the world. But let's stop for a moment and ask ourselves, is it God's desire?

God doesn't want us to dwell on the past. He wants us to maximize the present and control the future. So, what are you doing with the time you have? Do you remember bargaining with God for twenty-fours a day? Didn't He give us enough time to be successful daily? He absolutely did. Therefore, focus on maximizing it. There are characters in the bible who weren't ruled by time. Instead, they mastered time. These were the Sons of Issachar. The text says they had an understanding of the times and seasons. Understanding what you need to do with your time is what God desires; that we discern what needs to be prioritized.

This is not just doing extraordinary things, but doing the right things at the right time. These men understood what the times and seasons demanded. They knew the proper response to give. Furthermore, the bible says they understood what Israel was supposed to do at every given time. Do you know what you're supposed to for success? What does your business need to go into its next phase? What will earn you that promotion? Or cause your company's stock to rise?

Moreover, these men didn't just know when it was spring or summer; they knew the kind of crops to plant in summer and the kind of fruits that will appear in spring. They were like Joseph, who didn't just know that seven years of famine and plenty were ahead. He knew what to do to maximize those years.

Finally, 1 Chronicles 12:32 said something remarkable about these men. The bible says that two hundred chiefs and their kin were at their command. Can you imagine that? They were the leaders of their clan because of their ability to use time and not be used by time.

There are some contemporary people today, like the sons of Issachar, understand the times and the seasons. As a result, they are in command in various spheres. Undeniably, successful people are those who can manage their time and properly utilize it to produce the success they desire.

It was Steve Jobs who said, *"If you live each day as if it were your last, someday you'll be right. Every morning I looked in the mirror and asked myself: if today were the last day of my life, would I want to do what I do today?*

What a profound thing to say, it speaks of knowing how to use the time the right way. Steve Jobs was a great leader who utilized the gift of time God gave him. Indeed, those who can utilize time, using it to create possibilities for themselves and others are true leaders.

DANIEL: A MAN WITH A POWERFUL DAILY ROUTINE

Earlier, we saw that an excellent way to manage your time is to have a solid daily routine and stick to it. What daily routines do is: they eliminate distractions, enable prioritization, and help you form a habit of achieving set goals.

Without a daily pattern, you'll be disorganized and might leave off doing things that are important to your personal growth. This also helps us to maintain the discipline of doing the right thing at the right time.

A biblical character that exemplifies a leader with a powerful daily routine is Daniel. Although Daniel was a Hebrew, he was a top government official in Babylon. There were three governors and one hundred and twenty provosts who administered Babylon for the King, and he was one of the governors. Daniel, the bible said, was different from all the leaders in Babylon. The King recognized the glory in his life as the work of God's Spirit; he was so excellent that King Darius desired to make him the sole administrator of his entire kingdom.

When the other leaders of Babylon discovered this, they tried to ruin him, but they couldn't find anything against him. As a result of this, they hatched a plan. They were going to use his high level of discipline and integrity against him. These evil men got the King of Babylon to sign a decree stating that no one should offer prayer to any other God besides the King for thirty days, and those who went against this decree were to be thrown into a den of lions.

Meanwhile, Daniel had a daily routine of prayer. Despite how busy he was as one of the governors, he made sure he prayed three times daily. Nothing could shake this discipline, not even the fear of death.

The bible says in Daniel 6:10, *"Now when Daniel knew that the writing was signed, he went home. And in his upper room, with his windows open toward*

Jerusalem, **he knelt down on his knees three times that day, and prayed and gave thanks before his God, as was his custom since early days."**

I'm sure you know the whole story: how he was thrown into the den of lions but came out unhurt. The essential thing in our context is Daniel's discipline of having a daily routine, a specific time for prayer. He was a leader like you and probably even busier, but he had time to seek God. And he stuck to it even in the face of danger.

Another fantastic thing is, the bible recorded that this routine had been his custom since early days. This implied that before he became a governor in Babylon, he had this discipline. And even if his responsibilities increased, because he had a daily routine, it didn't affect his relationship with God.

JESUS: A LEADER WHO MAXIMIZED TIME

"All of us must quickly carry out the tasks assigned us by the one who sent me, for there is little time left before the night falls and all work comes to an end."

John 9:4 (TLB)

Jesus was the perfect example of a leader who valued time and knew how to manage. He was a leader on an important assignment: the liberation of all humanity. He knew that His life was for the accomplishment of the Father's will.

So, you can imagine how busy such a person would be. Yet, Jesus was able to maximize his time. No part of His life suffered because of His duties. He was able to utilize every single moment.

Do you remember Jesus was called a glutton because he had the habit of visiting people and eating with them? Where did He get the time to visit Zaccheus or Martha? How could he go to Peter's house to see his wife and Mother-in-law?

This was a man who spent his whole day speaking to multitudes and attending to their needs. Yet he had the time to train his disciples, appoint his apostles, and teach them about Kingdom-life. He was an incredible leader.

Let's take a look at some things Jesus said and did that shows his value for time:

1.   Jesus had a daily routine and allotted time to tasks – Jesus had a daily prayer routine and assigned certain times to this task.

"And in the morning, a long time before daylight, he got up and went out to a quiet place, and there he gave himself up to prayer."
– Mark 1:35 (BBE)

"Jesus often withdrew to lonely places and prayed." – Like 5:16(NIV)

"In those days, Jesus went out to the mountain to pray, and He spent the night in prayer to God" –Luke 6:12 (NIV)

"And when He had sent the multitudes away, He went up into a mountain apart to pray: and when the evening was come, He was there alone." - Matthew 14:23 (KJV)

The scriptures above show that Jesus had a daily practice of withdrawing from the crowd to pray. This wasn't something He did on impulse; He allotted time to prayer. How did I know?

In Matthew 26:40, Jesus invited His disciples to pray with Him at the Garden of Gethsemane, but they all slept off. When he found them sleeping, he asked Peter, *"Couldn't you keep watch with me for one hour?"* Jesus was saying that even if Peter was so tired, he could have allotted at least an hour to pray with Him.

What's more, even as He prayed, He was still conscious of time. I call that practical time maximization skills.

2.   He prioritized according to His divine assignment – The Bible records in John chapter 2 that Jesus, His mother, and His disciples attended a wedding in Galilee. While they were at the ceremony, the wine ran out, and His mother asked Him to do something about it. Our focus here is Jesus's response to His mother. He told her, *"My time has not yet come."*

136

We see in the book of John that turning water into wine was the first miracle that Jesus ever performed. In the context of this information, Jesus was saying that it wasn't yet time to show Himself as the Messiah. Who wouldn't want to be famous and influential?

However, Jesus' priority was His vision and assignment. His response is a clear indication that he prioritized his actions according to the fulfillment of His divine purpose.

3. **He had an attitude of redeeming time** – Jesus was always conscious of the fact that He was on an assignment. He had no time to take breaks, and He worked with a sense of urgency. In John 9:4, Jesus spoke of His death, He had only a short time to fulfill His ministry, and He wanted to maximize the time He had. Do you have this kind of approach to life? Are you passionate about fulfilling your life's assignment before the time runs out?

4 **He taught time management** – You can see that Jesus was a professional at time management. He didn't only do it; he taught it also. Jesus told a parable of 10 virgins to emphasize the need to prepare and wait for His return. In Matthew 25:13, Jesus explains the message in the parable, *"Therefore keep watch, because you do not know the day or the hour."* Jesus was telling them to use the time they had correctly. If they didn't know the day or hour He was coming, what did He expect them to do? He expected them to maximize every moment of their lives.

Can you say you're maximizing your life?

FINALLY...

"Making the most of every opportunity because the days are evil."

Ephesians 5:16 (KJV)

Joseph asked Egypt to save grain because the famine was approaching. Daniel prayed three times a day because he and his people were captives in a pagan land. Noah had time to build the ark. But soon enough, the hour for the building was over, and it was time to float in it. Jesus maximized time, for His time was short. The bible says that there is time for everything under the sun.

Your time is your saving grace. It is your defense form evil: recession, bankruptcy, disease, etc. and what you do with it now will determine what you become. You have to redeem the time, for great leaders are those who value time and also know how to maximize it!

LESSON 10

EVERYONE HAS POTENTIAL

(Great Leaders Don't Underestimate, They Understand)

Richard S. Wellins, co-author of *Your First Leadership Job*, once said, *"If you think your most important job as a leader is to write mission statements, set goals, or even increase revenue, you're focusing on the wrong metrics. Your most significant role doesn't involve your results; your job is to inspire your employees' results."*

Richard's statement is quite enlightening. It reveals that a true leader is interested in the productivity of His employees or followers. Great leaders believe everyone on their team has potentials and are willing to drive them to succeed.

Unlike what most bosses think, leadership is not just setting standards and making policies. It's not about digging round holes and sifting square pegs. It's not just about hunting for people who fit into our set-up, while others are discarded as soon as they cast shadows of doubt. This weak philosophy and lame mindset never leads to productivity and excellence. In truth, every man and woman out there has an element of unique potential. Some are hidden treasures, while others could be minefields.

Are you a leader fed up with incompetent people? Have you tried to improve an employee's efficiency and failed? Are you tired of moving in cycles of frustration and disappointment? Then, it's time to learn how to understand people and help them, rather than underestimate them.

Great leaders are not those who are only comfortable with competent and talented people but those who are good at spotting hidden treasures in everyone around them. So, rather than underestimate someone's ability to show-up and step-up, they

139

maintain a mental posture of acceptance and faith in everyone they meet. This is not just supposed to be every man's mental attitude, but it's a crucial part of a leader's *heartitude!*

WHAT ARE YOU SEEING?

"It is much more valuable to look for the strength in others. You can gain nothing by criticizing their imperfections."

Daisaku Ikeda

Merriam-Webster dictionary defines the word underestimate as *to estimate less than its actual size, quality or potential.* Simply put, to place too low a value on something.

First off, as a leader and influencer, you need to get to where you're able to see the goodness in others and do all you can to fetch their inner-diamonds. Whether by words or actions, you must be postured to encourage and motivate people, as you eagerly work to see their potential come alive.

I read the story of a young man who was going through difficult times. He didn't know what to do with his life. This fellow was without direction and focus, and it seemed like he was surely going to end up being a liability to his mother. Haven't we all been there one time or the other; in life's sticky mud, feeling stuck and unable to make progress, waiting while wasting?

When he returned home from college, one afternoon, he was hanging out at his mother's beauty salon when a respected old lady visited the shop. She took her seat, saw the young man, and couldn't take her eyes off him. Eventually, he caught her staring at him, and he felt awkward. Every time this young man looked in the mirror, he saw her behind him looking right at him. This woman saw something good and valuable in the young man, something he could not see in himself yet.

What did this Old lady see? What are you seeing? What kind of leader are you? Have you developed the attitude and nature that makes you look at your team and followers, and you could see great potential in them even before they get to see it themselves? Are you able to see hope and life in your followers even when others can't see them amount to anything?

After staring at the young man for a long while, the old lady finally said to him, *"You know, young man, you are going to travel the world and speak to millions of people."* Then, she wrote those words on a blue envelope and handed it to him. Instantly, her words communicated to his troubled heart, so he graciously accepted the envelope. Then, he put it in his wallet so he could carry it with him.

Today, Denzel Washington is one of the biggest movie stars in Hollywood. That confused young man has received two Golden Globe awards, one Tony Award, and two Academy Awards among others. Denzel once said in an article that the woman's words encouraged him when he was starting out as an actor. Guess what? Denzel still has that note. He became a success because someone had good eyes and could see his potential. What about you? Do you even lookout for potential?

MISSING YOUR LITTLE GIANT-KILLERS...?

Hey friend! Left to Jesse, there's nothing to see in little boys: Not big enough, tall enough, strong enough. Tiny, little boys can't compete! But why not? How about David? The Bible shows us Jesse, a father who couldn't identify his son's potential. Yet, can we blame Jesse? After six sons, another boy was born into the family of Jesse. He wasn't Daddy's favorite for anything beyond shepherding in the countryside.

Prophet Samuel came to Jesse's house to pick and anoint the next King of Israel. Jesse presented his six sons, his top-candidates. But little David was forgotten and left out of the big contest. He underestimated David, but God didn't. David lived to be the man after God's heart, and he became the anointed King of Israel. This boy faced and conquered the giant of Gath and cut him open with the warrior's sword. Great potential? No, daddy didn't think so!

Guess what! It's possible to be the Jesse in your business, home, church, school, board room and even personal life, ignoring that little giant-killer. Most leaders tend to focus on the best hands, the quality guys, and leave out others that might just need one recommendation, one word of encouragement, or one extra minute of your time to set them up for unimaginable success. Often, the gifted team member or employee you're looking for is close by but undiscovered.

LOOK AROUND YOU...

Many companies experience increased staff turnover year in year out. Although different factors can contribute to this, one way to reduce it is by learning to be more patient with your employees or followers and getting close enough to help them improve. As good as having competent hands in a team is, a leader must also seek ways to invest in people. Certainly, this can only be easy when you know them. Yes, when you know their strengths, understand their weaknesses, and empathize with their struggles.

A lot of great people (potentials) that are laid off in companies and organizations end up becoming pillars elsewhere. Have you wondered why? Among many likely reasons, understand that people become better versions of themselves when you value them and care for them. This makes them feel like an essential part of the organization. As a result, it increases their sense of commitment, and it encourages them to give their best to the job. Ralph Waldo Emerson said, *"Our chief want is someone who will inspire us to be what we could be."* Therefore, the key is winning the heart and loyalty of your followers, motivating them to stay and commit to the growth of your organization.

A FLICKERING CANDLE

"He will not crush the weakest reed or put out a flickering candle..."

-Matthew 12:20 (NLT)

Have you ever had a lousy employee? Or a team member who is the weakest link? How often have you thought about laying off such a person?

This passage of the scripture talks about the leadership of Jesus. As a leader, He never wrote people off, and the kind of people he chose in his team as his disciples, were the most unlikely bunch. Don't you agree with me that because of the sensitivity and impact of Jesus' assignment on earth, He should have been surrounded by *polished* individuals? He should have chosen men that are learned, exposed, wealthy and influential. Really, He should have gone to the Pharisees and Sadducees!

Conversely, Jesus went for men of untapped potential, who looked weak and undeserving: men like Simon Peter. Dr Myles Munroe said in his devotional and journal, *365 Days of Understanding, Releasing and Maximizing Your Potential,* that Simon means *the Flaky one,* depicting instability and weakness. Even his name, which was an accurate description of his personality, disqualified him; he was reckless and impulsive.

On a certain day, Jesus spoke to His disciples about His death and the things He had to suffer. Just in the middle of all that, Peter interrupted Jesus, urging Him to stop saying such negative words. What an audacious move? He failed to understand that this was Jesus's ultimate mission.

On another occasion, while Jesus was about to get arrested, Peter cut off the ear of a Roman soldier in a bid to defend his master. To top it all off, after being with Jesus for three years, this man profusely denied having anything to do with Jesus. Can you imagine such a person being your follower?

You would agree with me that he was clearly not the type of man to be called Peter (Rock). He was obviously unqualified to be the first leader of the church after the death and resurrection of Jesus. In our day, we would kick Peter out into the streets!

But, the most exceptional leader that ever lived, Jesus, saw beyond his inability, beyond his weaknesses, and his flaws. He saw a man that had the potential to carry His vision to the next level. Do you remember how Jesus told Peter that the devil tried to destroy him, but He prayed for Him not to lose faith? Jesus didn't reject Peter because of his many errors but was committed to nurturing the seed of greatness in him.

Jesus was a leader who saw people beyond the boundaries of their weaknesses. As a leader, you must aim to develop that little flicker of greatness in your followers. Though, not so bright and stable, there is a potential for it to glow.

At all times, be ready to help people find their voice in the noise, their fire in the smoke, and their motivation in the face of defeat. You may need to help others to put their pieces together, building greatness with the stones that life has thrown at them. Jesus believed in His followers. Do you have faith in your people?

Peter, the flickering candle burned brightly after three years of being with Jesus. By the empowerment of the Holy Spirit, he became the first leader of the early church. And after his first sermon, over three thousand souls repented and turned to the Lord.

See what the Bible said about Peter in **Act 5:15-16,** *"Then sick people were brought out to the road and placed on cots and mats. It was hoped that Peter would walk by, and his shadow would fall on them and heal them. A lot of people living in the towns near Jerusalem brought those who were sick or troubled by evil spirits, and they were all healed."* Can you imagine such a level of glory and brightness?

Just imagine the wealth of potential you have at your disposal. Welcome to the gold mine! Mind you, this is not a parasitic adventure. Real leadership does not mean you're at the top of the food chain. This lesson is not about sharpening the teeth of predators and the eyes of sky-hawks. People are not preys. Or how do you see human potentials? Little giant-killers waiting on you? Do you feel the urge to predate or to protect? Yes, you shouldn't put off a flickering candle, neither should you burn it out. So my question is, why are you digging for gold?

ATTITUDE OF LEADERS THAT BRING OUT THE BEST IN THEIR TEAM

It all begins with the right attitude. Richard S. Wellins said, *"Being able to bring out the best in others is a skill that involves just 10% natural inclination; the other 90% has to be deliberate."* Does this comfort you?

You don't have to worry about going to school to learn how to refine people, neither do you need a guide about understanding complex people. It basically begins by your readiness. Are you set to make it work? If yes, then you need to start cultivating some of these attitudes, make it a daily routine. There are times you may fall short and become judgmental, don't worry, persevere until it finally becomes your habit.

What then are some of these attitudes?

1.   **Paying attention to people's strength-** You see, no one wants to be underestimated, neither does anyone want to be in a place where his weakness is always talked about. Everyone wants to know they are doing something right; they want to know that their contribution is valuable. Great leaders identify and focus on the strengths of individuals in their team. They let them know what they are doing well, the area they are good at, and also give them the opportunities to use that strength and capacity.

The truth is, it will be easy to notice some people's strengths. However, for some others, you may need to take a step closer, pay attention, see what they enjoy doing, and notice the task they perform on time. You may just need to reassign then to that aspect of work so their strength can be refined while you encourage them by the side to work on their weaknesses. So, cultivate and help them improve talents and innate capabilities.

2.   **Empathy for your followers-** Great leaders understand and share the feelings of their team members. Knowing what they are going through, their struggles and the effort they put in place to become better. They are always ready to listen to what their followers are saying. They position themselves to see things from their employees' perspectives. For example, know why they come late, understand why they take longer to deliver on an assignment. This discovery helps you put yourself in their position and see if you would have done better. This knowledge helps you to know the areas they need improvement.

Also, in some emotional situations, a good leader will need to listen and respond with empathy, this will reduce tension. Because until all is calm, nothing productive can take place. The reality is, trying to understand your team members or employees will always drive better and more productive performance from them.

3.   **Creating a friendly environment-** People love expressing themselves. They love to be in a place where they are allowed to open up their thinking tank and explore ideas. A wise man once said, *"People who bring out the best in others give people permission to think, speak, and act with reasons."* Although, such leaders demand a level of intensity needed to achieve the set objective, yet they make allowance for mistakes and correct them in a friendly way. They make provisions for people to share their ideas. Trust me; you will be stunned by the revolutionary ideas lying dormant in your followers.

4.   **Delegating tasks and responsibilities-** Another way to bring out the best in people is to assign some duties to them. This makes them stretch beyond their comfort zone, and you will be surprised by what they can do. Great leaders allow their followers to take up roles. With time, as they start to earn small wins here and there, their confidence grows, and before long, challenges that seem insurmountable appear less daunting.

Great leaders understand that imbibing this attitude may not be an easy task. But in the long run, their determination to see the best in their team members will always keep them going.

GARBAGE IN…RECYCLE!

"Have a big enough heart to love unconditionally, and a broad enough mind to embrace the differences that make each of us unique."

-D.B. Harrop

Leaders must learn to accept all kinds of people. Although you may be tempted to lay them aside at first glance; yes! I know some people don't make a good first impression in most situations, but remember, your aim is to make them better, regardless of how crude they may be.

A great leader can accommodate the worst kind of people. He or she can take team members or employees that are weak, ignorant, naïve, or adamant and transform them into highly successful and efficient people.

This attitude is called developing a *recycle-mindset:* taking the waste on the garbage site and transforming it into a new, polished and admirable product. It works with people also.

While others are looking for those that are *made*, great leaders look out for those that can be improved upon to hit bigger targets. As a leader, whoever comes to you can and must be improved upon. It is a mindset that says, *"There is always a better version of everyone."*

Let me show you an example of King David in the scriptures. He was the most exceptional leader that Israel ever had. The only king that never lost a battle, not even one. He led the best team of soldiers to war and conquered lands.

But, something was unusual about how he set out as a leader. The Bible says in 1Samuel 22:1-2, *"When David escaped from the town of Gath, he went to Adullam Cave. His brothers and the rest of his family found out where he was, and they followed him there. **A lot of other people joined him too. Some were in trouble, others were angry or in debt,** and David was soon the leader of four hundred men."*

Did you see the pedigree and profile of those that came to David? ***A lot of other people joined him too. Some were in trouble, others were angry or in debt.*** These were the people that the king started with. What would have made David recruit such a group of people? They obviously lack direction for their life. How will they help David fulfill his vision? Capable hands should surround a man that been anointed king of the nation of Israel, right?

Israel, as at then, had many enemies, there was always one battle or the other. Yet a king chooses men without experience in fighting to work with him? There must be something else about King David that many don't know. He obviously knew the enormous task ahead of him, yet, he decided to bring different people together in his team. He was undeniably a leader that knew how to bring out the best in people. He saw high potentials in them, which others could not see. David drew them closer, trained them, and took them through the rudiments of what lay ahead.

However, after years of being under David's tutelage, these men became great men. Let' see what happened to a few of them;

One of them named Ishbosheth personally killed 800 men with a spear. 1 Samuel 23:8, *"These are the names of David's warriors: Ishbosheth the son of Hachmon was the leader of the Three Warriors. In one battle, he killed eight hundred men with his spear."*

Another one named Eleazar fought side by side with David against the Philistines. They defeated the army. Meanwhile, other Israelites soldiers ran away. 2Samuel 23:9, *"The next one of the Three Warriors was Eleazar the son of Dodo the Ahohite. One time when the Philistines were at war with Israel, he and David dared the Philistines to fight them. Every one of the Israelite soldiers turned and ran"*

Shammah also stood against the Philistines alone and defeated them. 2 Samuel 23:11-12, *"And after him was Shammah... And the Philistines were gathered together into a troop, where was a piece of ground full of lentils: and the people fled from the Philistines. But he stood in the midst of the ground, and defended it, and slew the Philistines: and the LORD wrought a great victory."*

Also, Abishai killed three hundred men with his spear. 2Samuel 23:18, *"And Abishai, the brother of Joab, the son of Zeruiah, was chief among three. And he lifted up his spear against three hundred, and slew them, and had the name among three."*

Now, these men were called *the Mighty Men of David.* Their result was unprecedented. But this was made possible because one man dared to be their leader. One man knew what it's like to see potential in people that would turn them to men that commanded outstanding result.

Who would have thought that these men had such extraordinary capabilities when they first came to David? Who would have thought that they would be relevant and eventually fit into David's purpose in life?

Therefore, I say, you have a part to play. If those crude members in your team would become productive, it begins with you been a leader that sees life and possibilities in them.

Consider a lumberjack who doesn't know how to sharpen his ax or a soldier who can't clean his rifle; the trees would be seen as rebellious, and the war would look like a nightmare. For every authentic leader must be able to sharpen his followers.

BECOME ALL THINGS TO ALL!

"Be the one who nurtures and builds. Be the one who has an understanding and a forgiving heart, one who looks for the best in people. Leave people better than you found them."

-Marvin J. Ashton

As I said earlier, one of the ways to bring out the best in people is to understand and appreciate them. Surely, there are always good things about people, and a great leader should always seek to praise their followers for what they do well. Most leaders wonder why their followers don't receive corrections with the right attitude. Let me ask, could it be that each time they hear from you, it's always about something they did wrong?

You may not get the best from people when it's all about their downfalls. But always try to begin with what they have done right, then their heart can be better prepared to receive the correction that will make them better.

To be a great leader, you must be deliberate about searching for the good in people; there are various ways to achieve that. You could create a time of the day when you take a walk around the office or where your team members are, remember you are out for the good, not the bad. When you notice someone doing the right thing, appreciate or reward it.

You could also designate people to do that on your behalf. Some organizations even have a day set aside for that; to reward those that do the right thing. When this becomes part of your leadership style, gradually, your team members will always be at their best. They ask themselves, *Is this the best I can do? Is this how far I can go? Can I still do better?* What have you done? You have set their minds on an auto frequency to always be better.

Someone who exemplified this attitude was Apostle Paul, in 1 Corinthians 1:4-7, the Bible says, *"I thank my God always on your behalf, for the grace of God which is given you by Jesus Christ; That in everything ye are enriched by him, in all utterance, and in all knowledge; Even as the testimony of Christ was confirmed in you: So that ye come behind in no gift; waiting for the coming of our Lord Jesus Christ."* Paul started by praising the Christians in Corinth. He deliberately searched out the bright side of these Christians. He mentioned the things they did right; he encouraged and appreciated them in the areas they performed well, and how God has helped them in various ways.

Seeing these verses of the scripture, you would think that was all he spoke about. On the contrary, Paul wrote to the Corinthian church to correct specific errors. For he had heard the news of divisions and sects among them; some pledged allegiance to Paul and others, Apollos. Instead of just condemning them and probably closing down the church; he preached to them, wondering what could have made them deviate in such a way.

Paul knew that there was more that could be done; it wasn't wise to throw away the child with the bathwater. He knew they could change for the better, and he made sure he addressed the issue.

Also, Paul accepted people as he met them; instead of trying to change them immediately, he adapted to their circumstances because the Apostle believed that through this medium, he could change them for the better through the gospel.

He said in 1 Corinthians 9:21-22, *"To those outside the law I became as one outside the law (not being outside the law of God but under the law of Christ) that I might win those outside the law. To the weak, I became weak, that I might win*

150

the weak. **I have become all things to all people, that by all means, I might save some.**"

Did you hear that he became all things to all men? That is the attitude that every leader should imbibe and develop. There are people in your team that you may need to take out for lunch and discuss ways to improve them. Some also require you to be firm with them, so that they can take their work seriously. It all boils down to understanding who they are and how best to approach them.

Paul was positive about these people because he knew that despite their sins, Christ could save them. He knew an encounter with Christ was the foundation they need for a transformed life. So, this meticulous Apostle mirrored their way of life to get across to them. He ate with them like Jesus ate with sinners and related to them in the way they could understand. What was the outcome? He was able to win their heart over, and they became Christians.

A LEADER WHO VALUES PEOPLE

In 9 lessons, we highlighted Jesus' excellent leadership pattern and gleaned truths from His lifestyle. But there is still more to learn about leadership from this exceptional leader of all times.

A remarkable thing about Jesus is that He knew what to do with raw materials and could transform something worthless into precious gold. Our perfect example, was always improving the world around Him; He turned water to wine, and when it was already wine, He said, this is my blood! That's on a lighter note, though.

However, we cannot deny the impact of Jesus's style of accepting people just the way they are, investing in them, and transforming them into world changers. So, how did Jesus do this? How is it that He didn't fire those who were weak or appeared incompetent? How did he turn garbage into greatness?

These principles you're about to learn are timeless, for Jesus is still applying them as He leads the church.

1. **He asked questions** - The bible records that the disciples of Jesus displayed unbelief and doubt on several occasions. For a Leader who placed great value on faith, He moved with an unbelieving bunch. They were such doubters that one of them was nicknamed *Doubting-Thomas.*

Jesus knew that every wrong behavior, every error, every weakness had a root. So, He often sought to know what was happening in the minds of His followers to understand their actions and help them grow.

One day, Jesus asked His disciples an important question in Matthew 16:15, *"He said to them, 'But who do you say that I am?'."* He desired to know what they thought of Him, and it turned out, only one of them had an understanding of who He was. Obviously, their ignorance was a significant part of their unbelief and lack of faith.

In the same way, learning to ask questions will help you know why followers or employees act the way they do. Maybe they don't understand the company's vision or their role in making it a reality. Moreover, you might get to discover their strengths and weaknesses.

Certain things Jesus did that are vital in how you can work better with your followers or your team, instead of underestimating or writing them off:

- Ask personal questions.

- Maintain good relationships.

- Accept people the way they are.

- Be accessible.

- Establish a system of getting feedback.

2. **Jesus always began with appreciation and encouragement** – Do you believe pointing out people's flaws makes them better? Are you the kind of leader that is always complaining? Jesus always put appreciation and encouragement before rebuke or correction. You

can see this in the letters written to the seven churches in the book of revelations.

Now, some of these churches deserved harsh reprimands – remember Jesus flogged people buying and selling in the temple – but He began by listing their strengths.

For example, Jesus had severe warnings for the Ephesian Church. Yet, He started by appreciating them: Revelations 2:3-4, *"I know you are enduring patiently and bearing up for my name's sake, and you have not grown weary. But I have this against you that you have abandoned the love you had at first."*

Wow! Talk about having exceptional leadership skills! Do you know how much applying this strategy can help your business or organization? Do you want to find out? Start with appreciation today!

FINALLY...

Are you a visionary? Are you hard working? Do you have unbreakable standards of excellence? Probably you're the type people would call a go-getter.

However, the duty of leadership is not about an abstract vision; instead, it's about a vision that serves people. Jesus knew this key secret, and that's why He told His disciples that He didn't come to be served but to help others. And as a leader, you owe it to those around you to nurture their potential and release it.

A wise man once said, *"A giant's ability to crush with his bare hands is not a sign of greatness, but his ability to protect with brute strength is."*

In the same vein, real leadership is not about choosing the best team or working with flawless people. It's being able to transform people's lives, taking them from where they are to where they should be. Therefore, great leaders are like miners; the dirt and grime do not repel them, neither do they underestimate, they dig for gold!

LESSON 11

SACRIFICIAL LEADERSHIP

"He who would accomplish little must sacrifice little; he who would achieve much must sacrifice much; he who would achieve much must sacrifice much."

James Allen

There are many excellent and remarkable quotes out there about what life is and what it is not. But can I just say that life is simply beautiful? Yes, amidst challenges and chaos, amidst dangers and darkness, amidst evils and societal ills; life presents a radiant beauty, outshining the ugliness.

Life's beauty is like the stars that wink from an inky-black night sky; the dullness of darkness spells gloom, but the twinkling of the bright lights make room for hope. Without a doubt, the beauty of life is hope, the guarantee of something better than yesterday and greater than today. A man can lose everything, but if he has life, he can regain all he has lost.

Think about the rush of being and the excitement of existing. Although there are many beautiful things in the world, they are ugly and undesirable without life. Imagine a wilted rose or a withered fig tree; their splendour and bloom was the life they once had.

No wonder the scripture says, *"A living dog is better than a dead lion."* A lion is the epitome of dignity and strength while alive, but all its splendour counts for nothing in the grave. Yet, life crowns the head of a wretched dog with the honour of hope. Life is more precious than all the treasures in the world.

However, there are those willing to give up something so beautiful and precious. Men and women who are ready to risk their lives to serve a cause greater than themselves. The Christian missionary, Jim Elliott, said, *"He is no fool who gives what he cannot keep, to gain what he cannot lose."* In other words, the person who can risk his life for something eternal; a purpose that goes beyond his own life, is wise.

From ancient times, there have been some forms of prices paid for one cause or the other. It might be to save a life or a group of persons'. Some sacrificed their comfort while others sacrificed their time and ambitions to champion a cause. But the highest price ever paid is the laying down of life for another.

Today, the world's history is replete with heroes and heroines who sacrificed their lives for their nations, families, friends and people they knew nothing about. We can't always pinpoint the motives behind these uncommon feats and courageous gestures. But we can say that some sacrifice their lives for patriotism, some for love for humanity, and others do it out of necessity. In every case, these people gave up their lives so that others can carry on with theirs. But what does this have to do with leadership? Everything.

LEADERSHIP IS SACRIFICE

It was John C. Maxwell, who said, *"The heart of leadership is putting others ahead of yourself."* Certainly, we can sum up what makes a great leader in one word – sacrifice! The strength to give your life for others is what immortalizes a leader; it is the greatest act of courage, the most exceptional heroism. No achievement is more significant. And understandably, it's a sacrifice that only a few are willing to make considering how difficult it is.

Leadership involves making a self-sacrificing commitment to others and a goal bigger than one's self. It involves trading tension for comfort, trading peace for turmoil. The true leader sees that the old story no longer works; recognizes that the new story has not yet been written. And has the courage to stand at the chaotic and dangerous place between the two.

Do you see leadership as an opportunity to benefit and enrich yourself, or you see it as an opportunity to improve the lives of others? Do you see leadership as an open buffet or a call to service?

"To whom much is given much will be required," said the Lord Jesus in Luke 12:48. Yes, much is required of leaders in terms of sacrifice. Simon Sinek once gave a talk that was titled "leaders eat last." While this topic is a little humorous, it sends a powerful message. Great leaders don't lead because of what they stand to gain; their pleasure is in ensuring that others gain bountifully.

Moreover, in the bid to emphasize the enormous sacrifice required in leadership, Gregg Thompson didn't mince words. He said, *"If you choose to lead, forget the notion that you will be idolized, universally admired, and richly rewarded. When you choose to become a leader, you're choosing a road plagued with failure, disappointment, confusion, and resentment. Your best decisions will be mocked. Your friends will abandon you, and loneliness will become your constant companion. Others will take credit for your great work, and you'll be blamed for their failures. Still interested in leading?"* Funny enough, after painting such a gory picture, he went on to say, *"I hope so."*

IT'S IN THE HEART

"The best leaders love the people they lead."

John C. Maxwell

"Greater love hath no man than this, that a man lay down his life for his friends."

John 15:13

Sacrifice and love are inseparable. A leader that will give his life or comforts for others must have his heart hewn in love because it is the driving force behind every sacrifice. For example, Mother Theresa loved humanity so much that she gave herself up. She once said, *"It is not how much we do, but how much love we put in the doing. It is not how much we give but how much love we put in the giving that."*

Genuine leaders are ready to sacrifice their lives to save others or to give them a better future. They are not afraid of death, neither are they too timid to defend a cause in which they believe. Attaining greatness as a leader means being ready to face dangerous oppositions, which is the accurate measure of a leader's strength.

In truth, what makes leaders exceptional is not just the ability to lead, but the ability to lead sacrificially. There is no success in leadership without sacrifice. Certainly, nobody got to Mount Everest by accident. You can fall off the top by accident, but you can't roll up by accident. Also, the higher the level of leadership, the greater the sacrifice.

Now you may ask, *"But is there an end to the sacrificing?"* Well, according to John C. Maxwell, *"You have to give up to stay up, and you stay on top by giving up consistently."* Leadership is a call to constant sacrifices.

Think about this for a moment: what kind of leader would you like to be led by? One who only thinks about himself? Or one whose only desire is to see you become better and stronger?

Sacrificial leaders don't force people to follow them; the strength of their character inspires, influences, and commands followership.

To better understand sacrificial leadership, we shall explore the lives of some selfless heroes who sacrificed their lives on the altar of patriotism and love for God and humanity. Truly, great leaders must be willing to make sacrifices.

LEADERS WHO MADE GREAT SACRIFICES

"Great achievement is usually born of great sacrifice and is never the result of selfishness."

Napoleon Hill

The Fugitive Slave Act of 1850 made for free enslavement of the blacks in American History. It was in the heat of this slavery that a brave woman called Harriet Tubman escaped as a slave and then became a conductor on the underground railway in rescuing several slaves. Harriet could have fled to another country to start a new life. But she sacrificed her freedom to give others a new beginning. She was a very significant figure in the liberation and freedom of about 300 slaves through this Underground Railroad.

In our world today, few people would risk their freedom or comfort for others. How many leaders know what empathy means? To put yourself in another person's shoes and love them enough to sacrifice anything of value.

Empathy calls for a great deal of selflessness, and Harriet Tubman displayed it in her actions. She had a conscience. She was unwilling to experience freedom while her people languished in bondage. Her priority wasn't her own life but that of others. Her sacrifice reminds me of another example of selfless sacrifice, which comes next.

When the *god-level ship* hit an iceberg in the open sea, four fearless engineers stayed at their duty post. At the same time, thousands of passengers tried to escape from the sinking vessel. They were able to keep the ship afloat for a longer time than it would have lasted. Because of their sacrifice, many people made it to the shore while their act of bravery took them gently down into the heart of the sea where the RMS Titanic still lies today. They literarily laid down their lives for others to live.

Again, these men show in their act of bravery, a great deal of selflessness. Can you imagine paying such a high price for others to live? I believe they knew they would die, but they found satisfaction in the knowledge that others would live.

Didn't they have families? Didn't they have something to live for? Wasn't life beautiful and precious to them? Yes, it was. But they valued the lives of others above theirs. Besides selflessness, they understood duty.

Throughout this book, I have emphasized that leadership is about followers. You are a leader because of the people that need your guidance and motivation. Your life is the service you render, and these next set of persons understood this correctly.

The *Immortal chaplains,* as properly called, were four World War II Chaplains who gave their lives for the people on the Dorchester ship on their way to Greenland. They gave out their life jacket before the ship finally sank.

When it comes to these chaplains, you can almost say that their sacrifice was foolish; this is because the instinct of the average schmuck would be to save themselves first. But they knew that they had a duty to secure the lives of those on board before theirs. I'm sure you're getting a better understanding of what Simon Sinek meant by *"leaders eat last."* Permit me to add, if there's no food left to eat, leaders should be content to starve.

Besides selflessness and duty, some remarkable leaders risked their necks for the sake of justice. In a world of corruption and compromise, such men and women are in urgent demand.

The United States of America was fortunate to have a leader who defied all odds to achieve equity and abolishment of the slave trade-Abraham Lincoln. His passion for the unification of American inhabitants, regardless of colour or race, was a leadership quality, for which the world would never forget him.

All the while, he knew he had adversaries from the slave states who saw him as a threat to their livelihood, and some wanted him dead. Still, he went ahead to declare justice and emancipation proclamation, which culminated in his assassination on April 14, 1865. President Lincoln's assassination made him a national martyr.

Think about the life of this great leader and realize that society's structure was built with the sweat and blood of men like Lincoln, who was willing to lay down his life for the greater good.

Here is another selfless individual who risked his life in the heat of the religious imbalance of the Roman Catholic Church. He is another man who fits into the category of dying while in the pursuit of truth. He stood against the Roman Catholic doctrine of selling *indulgences*- A belief that someone can be forgiven and be saved out of punishment by giving the priest an amount of money.

At that period, anyone who questioned the Pope; who was the final authority on matters of faith, was exiled or killed. Yet, Martin Luther caused a revolution by the *95 Theses* he published in the year 1517, risking his life to save others who were deceived and kept under the delusion of religion.

Martin Luther and the other heroes above remind me of a movie title: *A Few Good Men*. As I think about the title, I realize that it seems there are only a few good leaders today who would dare to pay the price for greatness. Who would risk their lives for others or even dare to die for upholding the truth and pursuing a just cause? Yes, there are a few good men, but are you ready to be one of them?

BIBLICAL EXAMPLES OF SACRIFICIAL LEADERSHIP

Abraham greatly loved his nephew, Lot, that he was willing to sacrifice his resources, his men, alliances and even his life to rescue him. Meanwhile, Lot had once shown a high level of disloyalty to Abraham, but this would not stop him from reaching out to him.

Three heathen kings had captured Abraham's nephew and his entire family. On hearing this, Abraham, not mindful of the risk or danger that could ensue from the battle against these three kings, launched out to save his nephew.

Just imagine one man with his army of three hundred men, trained in his own house, going against three different kings and their vast armies. Nevertheless, Abraham risked his life because of his love for Lot.

Abraham's sacrifice didn't begin that day, He had a track record of making selfless sacrifices for others; because of this, three hundred men were loyal to him and emulated his sacrificial lifestyle.

Earlier, I said, what commands followership and establishes influence is a leader's strength of character. Well, Abraham was such a leader. God appeared to him at a time to establish a covenant with him, the token of the covenant was the circumcision of himself and every man that belonged to his household. Whether a free man or a slave; everyman that was part of Abraham's massive family got circumcised.

Now, what could have made grown men yield themselves to experience such excruciating pain? What made them so loyal? What inspired them? I can assure you, it must be nothing but great and sacrificial leadership.

Another example is Moses, he had all the opportunities to emerge as the next Pharaoh of Egypt. His life's course was diverted when he discovered that he was meant to save the people of God. It was said of him in Hebrews 11:24-26, *"It was by faith that Moses, when he grew up, refused to be treated as the grandson of the King, but chose to share ill-treatment with God's people instead of enjoying the fleeting pleasures of sin. He thought that it was better to suffer for the promised Christ than to own all the treasures of Egypt, for he was looking forward to the great reward that God would give him."*

Pause for a moment. As you read all these things about Moses, what comes to your mind? Just one word: sacrifice! He was indeed a leader who understood the duty and responsibility of having people who believed in him and depended on him. He wasn't after what he could gain; in fact, he had rejected gain so that the Israelites could profit.

In Deuteronomy chapter 9, Moses recounted an incident that further showed his sacrificial heart. Here, the children of Israel had sinned against God by making a golden calf and worshipping it. Because of their actions, God had said to Moses, *"Let me alone, that I may destroy them, and blot out their name from under heaven: and I will make of thee a nation mightier and greater than they."*

Wow! Isn't this an excellent proposition for any leader? What would you have done if you were the one God wanted to magnify and bless? How many leaders would be sacrificial at this point? I tell you, only a few can resist such an offer.

But Moses wasn't the average kind of leader who would be enticed. Instead, being a selfless and sacrificial man, he utterly refused and pleaded on behalf of the people of God. This wasn't the only instance. Severally, Moses put his life on the line to save the Israelites from the destruction they continually brought on themselves.

On one occasion, when God would have destroyed the children of Israel, Moses did something extraordinary. He said to God, *"Yet now, if thou wilt forgive their sin--; and if not, blot me, I pray thee, out of thy book which thou hast written."* (Exodus 32:32). Can you imagine that? Moses put the people of Israel before himself. He was ready to lose eternally so they could gain and not the other way round. Are you such a leader?

Yet another leader in the holy book who made tremendous sacrifices and put his life on the line for others is the shepherd boy from Jesse's house. David rose to stardom, not by random voting or lobbying but by sacrifice.

In the face of severe opposition from Goliath, David risked his life without an armour: without a sword, and without a shield. All he took to the battlefield was a sling and five smooth stones. Doesn't this look like a sealed suicide mission? Is it even realistic? It is like marching into a lion's den with a rope as a weapon. Silly right?

But David, at that young age, had the heart of a sacrificial leader. His leadership journey began with leading sheep in the field, and on two occasions, he risked his life to rescue a lamb snatched by a bear and the other time, a lion.

No, David wasn't silly. He was a young man ready to put his life on the line for the freedom and victory of his people. Even when nobody believed in him, he was still willing to snatch his people out from the mouth of the oppressor.

There was no encouragement and no backup. The future of Israel depended on a young boy. Thank God he sacrificed his life at a time when the King and the armies of Israel were terrified.

At last, David's confrontation ended in victory as his stone sunk into the forehead of the formidable warrior and toppled the defiant giant. After the battle with Goliath, another internal battle began between him and Saul because the King became jealous of David's prominence in Israel.

Although Saul was out to kill him, David never desired to harm Saul, even when he had the opportunity. The truth is, it would have been in his best interest to kill Saul since he had been anointed to be the next King of Israel.

On the contrary, David chose to be on the run rather than murder Saul. Doesn't this show selflessness and sacrifice? He lived in a cave and spent his time providing leadership for the homeless and downtrodden.

While David was in desperate need of comfort and acceptance, he put his own needs aside to carter for the needs of the people who came to him in search of hope. So, we can say that selflessness and a sacrificial heart are two things that describe David's personality and leadership. Can someone say the same thing about you? What would you do if people's lives depended on your ability to sacrifice yours?

But before you answer that question, here's another biblical leader who sacrificed everything for her people.

It was just a few days before the total annihilation of her kin, including her uncle, Mordecai. Seeing the King without being summoned was an offense punishable by death, but this was necessary to reverse the decree that would destroy her people. Queen Esther's resolution to save her people, as fuelled by her uncle, was immovable. *"If I perish, I perish,"* she said. She looked her fears right in the face and grew valiant.

For Esther, there was no hope of coming back alive, but she was already committed. To her, the joy of seeing her people delivered was higher than that of being Queen. She did not use her status to gain immunity from the danger; instead, she took the full weight of the burden upon herself. Undeniably, she was selfless, she was sacrificial, and she was a great leader.

HE LIVED TO DIE

"…I am come that they might have life and that they might have it more abundantly."

John 10:10

The greatest sacrifice of all was made by a man who couldn't be repaid in any way for his great gift. Yet, He forfeited His glory and power, subjecting Himself to pain, shame, and death to die for people who rejected Him. Instead of aborting His mission because the people He loved were so undeserving, He loved them nonetheless and lived selflessly.

There was a need for someone to offer himself as a spotless (sacrificial) lamb for fallen man. And our Lord Jesus said, *"Here I am."*

In truth, Jesus had a way with words. He spoke with so much wisdom and authority that He could have avoided being crucified by convincing Pilate. Also, He could have easily defended Himself against the soldiers who arrested Him and saved himself from the accusations of the Pharisees. But Jesus' mission was to die for the sins of the world. He lived to die.

He thought about Himself and the gravity of the sacrifice he was about to make; He went to God in prayer and asked for the strength to align with God's will. All through his life and earthly ministry, everything Jesus did was to improve lives. He spent every waking moment preaching, teaching and healing the sick.

Severally, the bible mentioned that He had compassion for the people who followed Him. Close to the end of His life, Jesus made a statement that communicated His love and passion for humanity. He said in John 15:13, *"Greater love hath no man than this, that a man should lay down his life for His friend."* With these words, Jesus revealed that the driving force of His sacrifice was love.

THE FIRST MARTYR

Here is another fervent, selfless, and sacrificial leader; he was a devoted deacon of the early church. Accused falsely of speaking against the fundamental beliefs of the Jews, he was summoned before the Sanhedrin in Acts chapter 7.

Stephen presented before them an accurate and detailed defence against his accusation, and this got the council (rabbinical court of Judaism) infuriated that they led him immediately to be stoned to death. What do you think Stephen was supposed to do? Call down fire? But that was not what he did. Every stone landing on him could only break out streams of mercy and grace. Surprisingly, he started praying that the Lord would forgive those whose hands moulded his grave. What a selfless leader! Furthermore, he said, *"They know not what they do."* Are you kidding me? Wow! The faithful disciple of Jesus did not ask God to avenge him. After all, he was dying for a worthwhile cause. His words were exactly the words of Jesus on the cross.

164

He had learned from the master how to live a life of sacrifice. Stephen was the first martyr of the early church, the first person to die for the gospel of Christ. Stephen prayed for, not against his enemies even in the hardest moment. Neither did he pray for his rescue. Probably he knew that his death was essential to the fulfilment of the prophecies about the persecution of the church and to strengthen the faith of other believers. Undeniably, his life was a pleasing sacrifice to God.

THE PRIZE FOR THE PRICE

"And Jesus answered and said, Verily I say unto you, There is no man that hath left house, or brethren, or sisters, or father, or mother, or wife, or children, or lands, for my sake, and the gospel's, But he shall receive an hundredfold now in this time, houses, and brethren, and sisters, and mothers, and children, and lands, with persecutions; and in the world to come eternal life."

Mark 10:29-30

One day, after Jesus's disciples had successfully calculated the considerable measure of the sacrifice they had made to be His followers, they asked Him a question; they wanted to know the prize for the price. They had given up much to follow Him and wanted to know the worth of their sacrifice. And Jesus told them that what they had to gain was more than what they felt they have lost.

In a way, this is true concerning all the leaders listed above who made one sacrifice or the other. No heroic feat or selfless gesture was in vain. What Jim Elliot said, *"He is no fool who gives what he cannot keep to gain what he cannot lose,"* proved to be true in their lives.

So, you might ask, what did Harriet Tubman gain? Well, she helped to free many blacks from the shackles of slavery by her brave sacrifice; during the civil war, she served as a spy and helped free 700 slaves. Just as Jesus promised His disciples, she gained more brothers and sisters; if she hadn't returned to help the slaves after her freedom, she would have been all alone. Finally, Harriet wrote her name in the hall of fame by her sacrifice. Today, she's being remembered as an icon of freedom and extraordinary courage.

What about the Titanic engineers? What did they gain? Well, that day in April, when the *unsinkable* ship sunk, one thousand five hundred people died. But by their sacrifice, the engineers were able to help save hundreds of people. Records show that seven hundred and five people survived the wreckage. So, such a significant number of people had a second chance at life because of these selfless men. Aren't a hundred lives for one a great reward?

Likewise, the four chaplains who gave out their life jackets to others, would be reward by the many lives they saved that day. At least, they could go to their graves, knowing that they lived for something greater than themselves. How many people can make that claim? Can you? They became immortalized, and though dead, they live on in the hearts of those they saved. Their story will forever be told as an example of selflessness, love for others and sacrifice. Without a doubt, living is not what matters the most, it is living-on that does.

In President Lincoln's case, his assassination made him a national martyr. Abolitionists viewed him as a champion for human liberty. Republicans linked Lincoln's name to their party. Many, though not all, in the South, viewed Lincoln as a man of outstanding ability. Abraham Lincoln is revered till date as *one of America's most venerated heroes*, even among white Southerners. The crescendo came in 1922 with the dedication of the Lincoln Memorial on the National Mall in Washington, D.C.

What about Martin Luther, who stood alone against the Roman Catholic Church? Yes, his reward wasn't just temporal but eternal. After he risked his life to speak against the evils and the deceptions of the church, people began to think for themselves. Christians went back to the original teachings of the bible. His sacrifice began *the reformation*, and the Christian denomination known as the *Protestants* is the child of his struggles. Luther risked his life for the truth, and because of him, the Christian faith was preserved.

At this point, it is clear that sacrificial leaders are greatly rewarded for putting their lives at risk for others. And no, the prize for the price is not anything that can be measured or weighed on scales. It is beyond the material and temporal. Abraham's reward for risking his life for Lot was getting him back alive and winning the loyalty of his men.

In the same way, David's sacrificial lifestyle earned him fame and influence. Several years after defeating Goliath, David had men who were loyal to him and imitated his sacrificial lifestyle. On one occasion, two men risked their lives just to get him a drink of water.

As a leader, when you make great sacrifices, you inspire others to do the same. For instance, when the Hebrews heard that Queen Esther was on a fast and was risking her life for her people, they were inspired to do the same. And she was rewarded with the deliverance of her people.

FINALLY...

"Verily, verily I say unto you, except a corn of wheat fall into the ground and die, it abideth alone: but if it dies, it bringeth forth much fruit."

John 12:24

Jesus taught his disciples the mystery of a sacrificed life. He knew he wasn't going to be with them any longer, but he wanted them to understand his sacrifice. And not only that, he was preparing them to make the same sacrifice, which is what Stephen did.

Jesus died so many could live, while Steven died so that others could be strengthened and inspired to do the same for the gospel.

Great leaders understand that leadership is a call to sacrifice. The increase you desire requires sacrifice and so does the longevity of your vision. Jesus taught them that nothing lives on unless it dies first. Do you want to be a great leader? Do you want your influence to transcend generations? Do you want your name to live on? Then you have to be willing to die for others, die for a cause and die for the truth. Giving up your life, dreams and desires for someone else, is sacrificial leadership!

LESSON 12

PUTTING FIRST THINGS FIRST!

"Most of us spend too much time on what is urgent and not enough time on what is important."

Stephen R. Covey

"Wherefore seeing we also are compassed about with so great a cloud of witnesses, let us lay aside every weight, and the sin which doth so easily beset us, and let us run with patience the race that is set before us,

Looking unto Jesus the author and finisher of our faith; who for the joy that was set before him endured the cross, despising the shame,

and is set down at the right hand of the throne of God."

-Hebrews 12:1-2

Are you wondering if there's more to be learned about leadership? Of course, yes! There's more! Where do you live? What kind of house do you live in? Are you surprised I'm asking all these questions? Well, if you live where you have to use the stairs, then you'll understand why putting one leg ahead of the other makes a majestic walk up the case. What if you missed your steps on your way down a spiral staircase? Humpty Dumpty will show up to say HELLO!

Order and priority are rhythms of life. Listen to your heartbeat. Feel your breath, watch a parade, climb a ladder, try to swallow and breathe at the same time. Hey! Are you doing what I said? Wait! You should be reading. Looking up and down at the same time would be nice, but Ooops! You can't! Can you?

You see, there's only a thin line between life and death: that line is called a decision. We get to make it every day. Do you know that the choice not to decide is still a decision? So, let's face it! Every good leader is the one that can identify the thin-line of critical decisions and make the best choice based on PRIORITY!

A leader is like a watchtower soldier who stands sentinel over a city. Because of the sensitivity of a soldier's task, no one seems to understand priority the way he does. Beyond fatigue and sleep, he needs to stay awake. Boy, just like when a soldier is on duty, everyone can sleep with two eyes closed because they believe that there's someone—a leader—out there putting first things first.

A watchman's duty is to watch out for the enemy's attacks and send relevant signals to the city. That's first on his priority list. You see, it's the first on your priority list that will determine every decision you make as a leader. Would you decide to sleep if you're charged with such responsibility as a watchman? One day, a man asked his friend, If I called for help in the middle of the night and you're so dead-tired, would you choose me over a good night's sleep? He laughed and said, No, I would be too tired to hear your call. The truth is, you will always tailor your decisions towards whatever tops your priority list. To this man's friend, sleep comes before him on his priority list.

WHAT IF YOU HAD TO MAKE A CHOICE?

In April 2015, the 700 clubs featured the story of a man who was caught in a life and death situation, which explicitly illustrates the importance of priority.

The story goes like this:

In 2007, early September, a rancher named Sampson Parker took a short break from work to pick some corn on his farm. On getting to the farm, he switched on his corn picker and got down to business. Everything was working as it should, when all of a sudden, the corn picker got jammed.

According to Sampson, this wasn't the first time the machine had gotten clogged. Anytime this happened, he usually put off the corn picker. However, this time, he decided to leave the engine running because he thought the rollers would grind out the corn stalk that was causing the trouble.

So when the rollers couldn't do the job, Sampson grabbed the corn stalk and tried to pull it down. Unfortunately, this attempt failed, so he tried another means, which was to pull it up, but then disaster struck. **Instead of liberating the corn stalk from the machine, it pulled his hands into the rollers.**

This happened in a split second, and it caught Sampson off-guard. He was mad and terrified at the same time. He couldn't imagine how such a horrible thing could have happened to him. The rollers cut into his gloves and then, his right arm. Meanwhile, Sampson was grappling with his left hand, for anything he could use to jam the machine and free his right arm.

At that point, he turned to God in prayer and began to scream repeatedly for help. Gory and frightening thoughts flashed through his mind. He knew that if he didn't get free soon, he was going to bleed to death. Then, he thought about his wife and son coming home to find his lifeless body; this made him much more desperate to free himself from the rollers.

Fortunately, his eyes fell on the metal pin that connected the trailer hedge to the picker. He attempted using it to jam the engines, but his efforts proved abortive. After several attempts, it finally worked. Nonetheless, the gears kept grinding against the metal, and the friction caused some sparks to fall on the corn stalks on the ground. Soon, there was a fire outbreak.

Alas, this presented a more difficult situation to Sampson. He was stuck in the rollers, bleeding to death, and now, he was also in danger of burning to death. Suddenly, he realized that he had just one choice.

Quickly, he reached into his pockets with his left arm and brought out his dagger. The pain in his right arm was unbearable; the flames from the fire were burning into his arm and legs. Yet Sampson remembers the pain from the dagger to be the most intense– so intense that he passed out for a moment or two.

Sampson had to choose between burning to death and losing his right arm. Here, he knew that the priority was his life. Yes, he would be deformed for the rest of his life, but at least he would be alive. So, he began to cut into his right arm with the dagger; he cut flesh, nerves, arteries, and more.

Finally, when he got free from the corn picker, he ran away from the machine with pure joy and relief, shouting all the way, I'm free! I'm free! I'm free!

Now it looks absurd that Sampson was talking about freedom when he had lost his arm. But this rancher was looking at priority. At that moment, even if having complete limbs was important, his life was essential to him and his family.

This is precisely what priority is, and a true leader must learn to prioritize for the all-round benefit of his team, followers, colleagues, or employees.

Understanding how to prioritize tasks and responsibilities is a vital requirement for any successful leadership. It's not just about having an idea of what you need to do, but the best order to do them.

The greatest leaders of all time are the ones who paid attention to priority. From contemporary to biblical leaders, the ability to focus on the most important issues and relegate others to the background is what distinguished the wheat from the chaff.

Great leaders understand that, seeking immediate gratification by attempting to solve only the problems that seem the most pressing at the moment, does not produce long-lasting success. The ability to assess your responsibilities and determine what aspects would be most productive to tackle, and then go ahead to make it happen is the true stuff that makes for outstanding leadership.

LISTENING FOR THE CALL AMIDST THE NOISE

"Now in those days, when the number of the disciples was multiplying, a complaint arose from the Hellenists against the Hebrews, because their widows were neglected in the daily service.

The twelve summoned the multitude of the disciples and said, "It is not appropriate for us to forsake the word of God and serve tables."

- Act 6:1-2

Here is a story that has been mentioned previously, but still contains untapped truth and is relevant to understanding priority in leadership. Clean your shades and watch closely!

Remember, the early Church experienced an unprecedented increase, but with that increase came a challenge. You'll find that people can draw you into issues they could have solved themselves. So, more than ever, you need to learn to separate the call from the noise.

Can you imagine the Apostles of the early Church, including Peter being immersed in the big chicken soup that has to feed thousands of early converts? Yet, in addition to the ministry of the word and prayer—which was their original call; these men of God had to manage the stomach ministry of their rapidly growing congregation.

Talk of insatiable desires, we humans are indeed complex primates. As you would expect, the twelve Apostles had to choose between spreading themselves too thin on the array of daunting responsibilities. Perhaps they wanted to be like Jesus, don't you think? They probably felt that as leaders, they should go beyond spiritual service to other areas, like food services. So, out of their busy schedule of attending to the people's spiritual needs, praying for them, and teaching them the word, these men still got involved in serving tables.

As time went on, a problem arose in the Church that served as an eye-opener: it helped the Apostles put things in perspective and identify their priority. Although the leaders of the Church were in charge, the food wasn't properly distributed. Soon, the Grecian Jews began to complain about their widows being neglected in the daily distributions.

They realized that for a while, their action kept the Church together, but not anymore.

The truth is, there is a level of growth that a system will attain that would require the leaders to delegate their former responsibilities and focus on more crucial matters. Likewise, it was all right for the Apostles to get involved in other matters while their number was few. But as the Church grew, they realized that serving tables wasn't their priority.

Do you know what the Apostles did? They simply appointed men to fill up that space while they faced their major kingdom assignment.

The Bible says in Act 6:3, "Therefore select from among you, brothers, seven men of good report, full of the Holy Spirit and of wisdom, whom we may appoint over this business." They realized that the reason the people came to them in the first place was because of the ministry. And that the Church existed to satisfy their spiritual needs before their physical needs.

Imagine if they successfully satisfied the congregation by devoting themselves more to serving tables. Yes, they were trying to avoid division among the Christians, but neglecting their duty would have caused a decline in followership. Probably, the early Church would have collapsed. On the contrary, the leaders knew how to prioritize.

This is what they said to the other believers, Acts 6:2 & 3, "Then the twelve called the multitude of the disciples unto them, and said, it is not the reason that we should leave the word of God, and serve tables…But we will give ourselves continually to prayer and the ministry of the word."

What do you think was the outcome of their decision to pay attention to priority?

Firstly, the Bible says in Act 6:5, "These words pleased the whole multitude…" In other words, peace and unity were restored in the Church. Everybody was satisfied with the leadership once again.

Secondly, in Act 6:7 the Bible says, **"The word of God increased,** and the number of the disciples multiplied in Jerusalem exceedingly. A great company of the priests were obedient to the faith."

Behold the power of priority! The word increased: there was a better understanding of the word, and more people heard the gospel. Their numbers would have reduced because of strife increase, however, by delegating their previous duties, the Apostles created room for more leaders, which meant more influence and scope of coverage for the early Church.

Above all, many people became obedient to the faith. Hence, the simple decision of the Apostles to put first things first brought about all-round success.

PRIORITY WILL FUEL YOUR PASSION

"It is the responsibility of leaders to make tough decisions based on priorities."

John C. Maxwell

"Yea doubtless, and I count all things but loss for the excellency of the knowledge of Christ Jesus my Lord: for whom I have suffered the loss of all things, and do count them but dung, that I may win Christ."

Philippians 3:8

There's a remarkable leader in the Bible whose timeless influence cannot be denied. He was a man of tremendous focus and passion. His name is Paul.

When Jesus commissioned Paul to be an Apostle to the Gentiles, part of his marching orders was that he would suffer many things for the sake of Jesus.

Today, it is believed that Paul did more than any of the Apostles in his time. He had incredible results in his ministry, and yes, he suffered just as Jesus had told him. Nonetheless, he wasn't deterred or discouraged. Rather than allow the hazards of being a missionary discourage him, he puts first things first. He sets his priority above his hardship.

In 2Corinthians chapter 11:24-29, Paul lists some of the things he had to go through for the sake of the gospel: "Of the Jews, five times received I forty stripes save one. Thrice was I beaten with rods, once was I stoned, thrice I suffered shipwreck, a night and a day I have been in the deep; In journeyings often, in perils of waters, in perils of robbers, in perils by mine own countrymen, in perils by the heathen, in perils in the city, in perils in the wilderness, in perils in the sea, in perils among false brethren; In weariness and painfulness, in watchings often, in hunger and thirst, in fastings often, in cold and nakedness. Beside those things that are without, that which cometh upon me daily, the care of all the churches. Who is weak, and I am not weak? who is offended, and I burn not?"

This zealous Apostle of Jesus experienced a plethora of bad incidents that would have drained the passion of any mortal man. Despite all the challenges he faced and pains he went through, he was able to survive and thrive because his life wasn't a priority to him.

Wow! Doesn't this sound a little bit extreme? What is more important than life?

Well, Paul's priority was to know Christ and win his heart. To him, this was worth more than his life. And this was where his zeal and passion for the gospel emanated from. In fact, he told a particular church that if he lived, it was for Christ's sake, and if he died, it was gain; because he would finally be with Christ.

No wonder he made this baffling statement in Philippians 3:8 "...I have suffered the loss of all things, and do count them but dung, that I may win Christ."

In effect, Paul was saying that at a point, he had to come to a decision. He had to choose between preserving his life and the things that meant so much to him, and doing God's will. And even if he knew that following Jesus would cost him everything, it was His priority. So whatever he lost became secondary and irrelevant compared to preaching the gospel and living for God.

Moreover, there was a period in Paul's life, where he had to choose between freedom and imprisonment. Yet he chose what he felt was a priority. Act 21:11-13, "And when he was come unto us, he took Paul's girdle, and bound his own hands and feet, and said, Thus saith the Holy Ghost, So shall the Jews at Jerusalem bind the man that owneth this girdle, and shall deliver him into the hands of the Gentiles. And when we heard these things, both we, and they of that place, besought him not to go up to Jerusalem. Then Paul answered, What mean ye to weep and to break mine heart**? for I am ready not to be bound only, but also to die at Jerusalem for the name of the Lord Jesus.**"

In the scripture above, a Prophet named Agabus warned Paul not to go to Jerusalem because if he did, he would be arrested. But Paul insisted on embarking on this journey, for he wanted to preach the gospel, and nothing was more important to him than that.

Paul's nark for focusing on priority can also be seen in his statements about marriage: 1Corinthians 7:8 & 32(CEV), "Here is my advice for people who have never been married and for widows. You should stay single, just as I am...I want all of you to be free from worry. An unmarried man worries about how to please the Lord."

Paul's reason for remaining single was because he wanted to be completely devoted to preaching the gospel and serving God.

Since Paul was able to identify what was most important to him, he became more successful and covered more ground than any of the other Apostles. He is believed to have written two-thirds of the New Testament.

CHALLENGE YOUR PRIORITY

When Nokia was going to be sold to Microsoft, following astronomical business losses and what could be referred to as a brand failure, the CEO ended his speech with the famous line, "we did not do anything wrong, but somehow we lost." Entrepreneur.com listed failure to adapt to new information as one of the greatest mistakes in prioritizing. Had they chosen what was important over what was vital?

After years of delivering quality mobile devices and making a name, it would naturally become an instinct to seek to protect the very nature of what has led to such household-level success. However, the heartbreaking sale of the beloved tech company revealed an important lesson in leadership choices.

While it is **important** to guard the landmarks, it is **vital** to ensure that the future of the environment is secured by a constant acquisition and response towards new information. The company was sold at a time when it could have made a whole lot of money if only the initial reputation of the brand – **which was important** -- had not been prioritized over the more dominant new operating systems in the market **(which was vital). In contrast,** the company could have utilized its name as a point of leverage to offer the new operating system from higher ground.

Hewlett Packard, also known as **Hp**, was formerly a utility company, which gradually became known across the globe for producing personal computers. From this, we glean that another important skill for making decisions as a leader is the ability to understand that reputation is flexible.

Certainly, it is about knowing that the thing for which you have been recognized does not need to be what you stick with until the end. A company's reputation is important, but after it has been firmly established, other things would become vital to the longevity of that enterprise. Nokia totally misplaced its priorities, and they lost.

You need to understand that leadership is mostly about decisions. History is full with accounts of leaders who set varying priorities for themselves and for their people. These priorities went on to affect their followers in ways that were positive and, in some cases, not so much.

But what makes a leader truly great? I believe it is the ability to always determine and choose, what is vital, not what is important or pressing. A leader must understand the best step to take in achieving every cause he/she embarks upon. Most times, a great leader is the one who can identify a task and then direct all his/her attention to it as though nothing else matters.

For instance, there's an intriguing story in the Bible that illustrates the difference between what is a mere distraction and what is important. This tale is about a man who was running from his maker. God had given him an assignment that he disliked, and he thought the solution was to take to his heels in the opposite direction. Bad move, right?

He went to a town named Joppa, where he boarded a boat off to Spain. How hilarious! Didn't he remember who made the seas? Had he forgotten that God created the whole earth and that no one could run from Him?

Because of Jonah, God sends turbulence on the sea. The Bible puts it this way, Jonah 1:4-6, "But the LORD made a strong wind blow, and such a bad storm came up that the ship was about to be broken to pieces. The sailors were frightened, and they all started praying to their gods. **They even threw the ship's cargo overboard to make the ship lighter**. All this time, Jonah was down below deck, sound asleep. The ship's Captain went to him and said, "How can you sleep at a time like this? Get up and pray to your God! Maybe he will have pity on us and keep us from drowning."

Now, when the storm started, the passengers aboard the ship went into panic. All the sailors began to pray to their gods for help in their terror. At that moment, they had only one prevalent thought – survival. It was the only vital thing!

So they decided to throw their goods overboard to lighten the ship's load. Yes, the ship's cargo was important to them. Some of the goods they threw overboard were food that would've sustained them throughout their journey. Probably, other items were goods they had bought for trade. However, they were caught in a life and death situation, and what was vital at the moment was life.

Meanwhile, the gentleman who had put them in such a precarious situation was sleeping soundly below deck. Finally, the Captain stomped into his cabin and roused him out of sleep. The sailor was furious that someone could be fast asleep when men were fighting for their lives. They needed more people to pray to their gods, so Jonah was hoisted on deck to help.

As time went by, they consulted among themselves who or what could be the cause of such a storm. It was at this point that Jonah came out of hiding. He confessed to be the reason for their distress. And when they heard this, the sailors asked how they could appease Jonah's God; his answer surprised them. Jonah 1:12-15, "Jonah told them, '**Throw me into the sea**, and it will calm down. I'm the cause of this terrible storm.' The sailors tried their best to row to the shore. But they could not do it, and the storm kept getting worse every minute. So they prayed to the LORD, 'Please don't let us drown for taking this man's life. Don't hold us guilty for killing an innocent man. All of this happened because you wanted it to.' Then they threw Jonah overboard, and the sea calmed down."

At first, when Jonah asked to be thrown aboard, the sailors ignored him. They considered it unnecessary and even extreme. But as the storm grew worse, they had to pay attention to what was vital. Certainly, they had to save the lives of many, even if it meant endangering the life of just one person.

Here, the passengers on the ship were faced with another decision. To choose their lives over the ship's cargo had been easy. But then, in Jonah's case, they had to choose between what was vital and what was important.

More often than not, you can locate priority by identifying the choice that has direr consequences than the rest. In such circumstances, true leaders are those who can differentiate between what's vital and what's important. A great leader puts first things first; this aids a sequential and unique result they desired.

HOW TO PUT FIRST THINGS FIRST

Stephen R. Covey once said, "As a leader, the key is not to prioritize what's on your schedule, but to schedule your priorities." That is, defining what is important and making plans to achieve them. It's not about how busy you are as a leader, but how effective and true you're to the goals of the organization.

1.   **Keep tabs on tasks and organize them based on priority:** There's a saying that the faintest ink is better than the sharpest brain. If you think you can have all your activities in your mind, then you would likely leave important tasks undone. It doesn't take long to write down your activities. Some call it a to-do-list. As you are penning the tasks, your mind begins to set them in order, so you can know what to concentrate on and do first.

2.   **Tackle the difficult tasks first:** It's always tempting to unconsciously move the difficult task to a later time. But it's more effective to handle the difficult tasks first. With this, your workload becomes lighter, and the rest of the day becomes less stressful because you've gotten over the most complicated and time-sapping task for the day.

3.   **Know your most productive moment:** It's important to understand the time of the day when you are most productive. This helps to place more important and urgent tasks at this time. In the same vein, you can delegate tasks that are less important to your least productive moment.

4.   **The Eisenhower Matrix:** The former President of America, Dwight D. Eisenhower, once designed a priority matrix for effective leadership. According to him, as a leader, if an assignment is urgent and important, it should be done first. If it's not urgent but important, it should be noted in your schedule. But if it is urgent but less important, it should be delegated.

However, Eisenhower advised that any task that's neither urgent nor important should be removed from your schedule and downright from your mind.

5.   **The Three R's of priority:** John C. Maxwell, in his book, *The 21 irrefutable Laws of Leadership*, revealed what he calls the Three R's of priority. And these are requirement, return, and reward. Therefore, to ensure that you are focusing on what's most important and avoid distractions, you need to ask three vital questions.

First, what is required? Second, what produces the most significant return? And lastly, what brings the highest reward? Your ability to ask and answer these questions will determine the success of your firm and the efficiency of your team, employees, or followers.

FOCUS ENHANCES CLARITY

"The light of the body is the eye: if therefore thine eye be single, thy whole body shall be full of light."

Matthew 6:22

When a man knows he only has thirty-three years to fulfill a global assignment that will impact on mankind, from the word go, he will set his priorities right, and keep his eyes straight.

This was the example of Jesus. His three years of ministry were met with distractions. Starting from the temptation at the beginning of His journey to final prayer at Gethsemane. Yet, He remained a leader to sit and learn from.

He exemplified a leader with a busy schedule, yet chose what was necessary.

The Bible says in Luke 5:15-16, *"News about Jesus kept spreading. Large crowds came to listen to him teach and to be healed of their diseases. But Jesus would often go to someplace where he could be alone and pray."*

You may wonder why Jesus sneaked away into the wilderness. I thought He came to the world to preach and heal and deliver. What happened in this city?

Earlier, Jesus had healed a leper, and the man was made whole. Then the people began to look for Him. Have you been in a situation where you allowed the demand of the people to determine your decision? Have you abandoned what is important because people need your attention? Rather than being moved by the high demand for His attention, Jesus chooses what was important. He went quietly to pray. He knew that He has no ability of Himself except God was with Him. Jesus knew that there is more to do than the time to do it. So, He didn't trade his intimacy with God for activities and miracles. He knew when to move close to the people and when to withdraw from them.

JESUS: SEPARATING THE NOISE FROM THE CALL

"After the people had seen Jesus work this miracle, they began saying, "This must be the Prophet who is to come into the world!"

Jesus realized that they would try to force him to be their king. So he went up on a mountain, where he could be alone."

John 6:14-15

How would you feel if you are called upon to be a king or occupy a prominent position in your office or even your country? I guess you will jump at it, right? Well, the best of us will.

But Jesus used this also to exemplify focus and seeking priority in all areas. He had just fed over five thousand people with excess leftovers. It was indeed a moment of prominence. The people have never seen it done in such a fashion. So they felt the best way to secure their future was to make him king. *If this prophet can become our king, no more hunger in the land,* the people thought to themselves.

But Jesus had a higher focus. His priority was set, and the attractive offer from the people would not distract Him. Rather than following the hail and praise of the people, His priority was to seek the honor that came from God and not from men.

FINALLY, …CAN I HAVE YOUR ATTENTION?

Going forward, what will be your next move? Remember that, as a leader, you're in a strategic place to craft the future of your business or company. Your decision or indecision will have a ripple effect on you, your business, and the team. Therefore, you have to evaluate your priorities and pay attention to what matters the most. Nobody wins, running a decisive direction.

Put off your pajamas, pull on the boot, drop the baggage, you've got a race—a finish line ahead of you. So, I challenge you to focus- fight, focus- prioritize, focus- finish; you deserve to win, and you will, when you put first things first.

God Bless You!

LESSON 13

LEVERAGE ON DIVINE ADVANTAGE

Man has a dual residency. This is so because he interacts with two realms at the same time. Yes, there are two realms man relates with daily—the realm of the spirit and the realm of the physical. In the book of **Genesis 1:26**, we read God's intention to create man in His image. It says, *"And God said, let us make man in our image, after our likeness..."* Remember, this was after God created the physical realm in which man was to live.

Now, the question is, *what is the image of God?* John 4:24a makes this clear. *"God is Spirit..."* If God is spirit, what He made in Genesis 1, must be a spirit like Him. Nevertheless, because of the physical world in which man is to live, lead, and rule, he needed a body. Our leadership mandate didn't begin in the physical realm. Leadership is initiated from the heart of God, who is the father of all spirits.

Hence, the reality of the spirit realm supersedes the physical realm—the spiritual rules the physical. From careful observation of the creation of man, it's clear that the physical realm finds its source in the spiritual realm. *"...the world was created by the Word of God, so that what is seen was made out of things which do not appear."* It means that nothing finds expression or beginning in the physical realm without an influence of the invisible realm.

Sincerely, why do you think people get into mysticism, cultism, and metaphysics? These are all pointers to the limitations of the human senses in untying the Gordian knots of life. We are spiritual beings. In truth, every leader that ever lived a life of extraordinary impact, were people who leveraged on the advantages of a realm that transcends their wisdom.

BENEATH THE SURFACE

Beneath the surface of the growing technology and wisdom of man is supernatural influence and inspiration. When you talk of leadership and harnessing the advantages of the unseen realm in achieving maximum results, both the secular and the religious sectors of life resort to spirituality, even some scientists, who debated and doubted God's existence, now realize that life is beyond electrons or protons in an atom.

For instance, Ian I. Mitroff, a Business Professor, while researching companies for his book *A Spiritual Audit of Corporate America*, discovered that *"spirituality could be the ultimate competitive advantage."*

More so, from biblical history to the ancient philosophers, and archives of other world leaders, it is evident that they utilized spirituality in attaining greatness. I mean, talk of Jesus, Saul, David, Peter, Paul, and Plato, Aristotle, Sun Tzu, Abraham Lincoln, Martin Luther, Marcus Aurelius, Shakespeare, and Gandhi. These were leaders who leveraged the spiritual advantages available to them.

Now, it's crucial to note that spirituality doesn't necessarily imply religion. However, every religion has spirituality at its core. The Christian religion has a set of principles that guides its followers. Muslims believe in the five pillars. Buddhist in the Eightfold path; Hindus sustain a set of principles called Sadhana, while secularist practices a form of reflection and meditation to enhance their effectiveness. The point is, spirituality provides a world of advantage for leaders from all spheres of life. Now imagine how disadvantaged and vulnerable you would be as a Christian leader who does not leverage his/her spiritual heritage and advantage.

MEN WHO VALUED AND UTILIZED SPIRITUAL ADVANTAGE

Having spiritual support and an advantage is of utmost importance in leadership. For instance, Saul was the first king of Israel, who ruled under the spiritual oversight of Samuel. He enjoyed spiritual guidance early in his reign as the King of Israel. Meanwhile, before the death of Samuel, Saul had outlawed witchcraft and sorcery in the land.

However, after the death of Samuel, a great battle arose against the land of Israel by the Philistines. Saul gathered all the army and camped at Gilboa. But when Saul saw the Philistine army, he became frightened and went back to God for divine guidance and instruction.

By the way, there will be times in leadership when you will be at your wit's end, and your strength, intellect, planning, prowess, strategy and ability will fail. Saul was in such a quagmire. The only option was a spiritual source of answer and instruction. Saul went to inquire of the Lord what he should do. But he already lost his spiritual advantage because of disobedience.

After Saul lost the advantage of divine direction, he had to consult the same witches and mediums he had once banned from the land. The bible said in 1 Samuel 28:7, *"Saul then said to his advisers, find a woman who is a medium, so I can go and ask her what to do."* This shows the importance of gaining spiritual wisdom and foresight as a leader. Before making decisions or taking deliberate steps that would affect a whole nation, Saul needed a supernatural answer. In the same vein, as a leader, you cannot afford to make insensitive decisions, knowing it will affect a wide range of persons.

Saul exemplified how weak and helpless a man (King) can be without spiritual advantage. In truth, some people get to the end of their rope before they suddenly realize they need a greater force.

Here is another example of a leader who valued and harnessed the divine advantage available to him despite the impossibilities staring him in the face. David came back from a battle after three days to see his city and family raided by the Amalekites. David and his armies wept for their loved ones until they had no strength to weep; all hope seems lost.

Now, to make matters worse, his men were ready to stone him because they blamed him for their misfortune. You see, in leadership, your followers will always believe you know what to do and the best way to overcome all odds. However, after putting so much trust in you and your humanity surfaces, they will immediately see you as that weak leader that is helpless.

Can you imagine that David, a leader they all revered, obeyed and loved, had now suddenly become a target? What did David do in such a critical and helpless situation? I'll tell you! He leveraged on his supernatural advantage. 1 Samuel 30:6b and 8a, *"But David strengthened himself in the Lord... And David enquired of the Lord..."* David turned to the right place and got the right answer from the Lord before embarking on the battle of recovery. He pursued, overtook, and conquered. Why? He leveraged on the Divine advantage.

Moreover, what was the secret to Uzziah's prosperity? What did he do differently that guaranteed his blessings and prosperity? 2 Chronicles 26:5, *"He set himself to seek God in the days of Zachariah, who instructed him in the fear of God, and as long as he sought the Lord, God made him prosper."* The secret to a life of guaranteed blessings as a leader, is your connection to God. Why is seeking God a key to prosperity and abundance? The reason is that you will regularly walk in wisdom and direction that ensues from God. As long as he sought God, the source of wisdom, his prosperity was established. Leveraging on supernatural advantage guarantees your success.

MIRACULOUS INCREASE; MYSTERIOUS RESULTS

One of the disciples of Jesus, whose relationship was characterized by deep and clear evidence of a man who leveraged on divine advantage, was Peter. He seized every opportunity to connect to the supernatural realm. Peter was a professional fisherman before he met the Lord. He knew all the skills to use and get fishes out of water. Above that, Peter understood timing in getting the most out of his profession; he knew the most pleasant time to get the fishes in multitude (at night). However, with all the skills, tactics, sense of timing, hard work, and diligence, Peter got to his breaking point. What saved him and brought miraculous increase: mysterious results? Peter connected to the realm beyond his senses. Luke 5:5-6, *"And Simon answering said unto him, Master, we have toiled all the night, and have taken nothing:* **nevertheless at** *thy **Word** I will let down the net. And when they had this done, they inclosed a great multitude of fishes: and their net brake."*

Have you also come to the point of putting several efforts into your profession, and all you have is nothing? Or you just get to cross your hands at some point and say to yourself, *it's ENOUGH?* It's time to tap into the wisdom of Peter: *nevertheless at thy word.* Peter took advantage of the living Word of Christ that makes things that be not as if they were. Without any controversy, the spiritual rules the physical. The same river they thought had no fish, produced a great catch and overflow. Inevitably, when you connect to the unseen realm, the results are always mysterious and unexplainable.

Likewise, how do you explain money in the mouth of a fish? We can easily relate to money in a bank, in a safe or in a purse. But money in the mouth of a fish? Come on! Isn't that mysterious?

Well, this is how the story goes: Jesus and His disciples needed to pay tax and had no money with them at the time. Probably Judas Iscariot went out with the bag of coins. So, what did Jesus do? Start complaining? Or stand there confused? NO! He connected to the realm of increase and sufficiency immediately. He instructed the disciples on what to do, Matt 17:27, *"Notwithstanding, lest we should offend them, go thou to the sea, and **cast an hook**, and take up **the fish that first cometh up;** and when thou hast opened his mouth, thou shalt find a piece of money: that take, and give unto them for me and thee."* As a leader, you must know how to respond to dark moments while leading the people. Jesus leveraged on the unseen realm to access what He needed at the time. Leaders must have foresight and insight into how a problem should be attended to adequately.

KEYS FOR LEVERAGING ON DIVINE ADVANTAGE

"And He said, 'to you it has been given to know the mysteries of the kingdom of God, but to the rest it is given in parables, that 'Seeing they may not see, and hearing they may not understand.'"

- Luke 8:10

Jesus revealed to His disciples that as those who believe in Him and have entered into the dispensation and rule of God's kingdom, they had certain privileges. One of these privileges was to know and understand the mysteries of the Kingdom of God. They would have unlimited access to the wisdom of God.

In other words, they would be able to learn, master, and harness God's ways to give them an edge over the natural realm. No wonder the bible, in Psalm 82:6, says, *"I have said, Ye are gods; and all of you are children of the Most High."* Therefore, as a leader who believes in Jesus, God wants you to know the mysteries and divine secrets that will equip you to leverage on divine advantage.

1. **Engaging the mystery of spiritual oversight and mentorship:** Spiritual oversight refers to a minster's duty and authority for the people God has set him over. He is to watch over them as his spiritual responsibility to God. Because God has authorized him, only those who align with him will access God's blessing.

    While Peter was speaking to some elders and leaders of the early church in 1Peter 5:2, he said: *"Feed the flock of God which is among you, taking the oversight thereof…"* Now, this great Apostle likened God's people to sheep by calling them flock. This was to convey his message to these leaders efficiently. They were to do the work of shepherds; provide protection and nourishment for the community of believers they were accountable for. It so happens that as a leader you belong to a flock, and you have someone who God has made your spiritual overseer. According to God's Word, your prosperity and progress are linked to your alignment with this servant of God. Take a look at what the bible says about this in 2 Chronicles 20:20, *"…Believe in the Lord your God, so shall ye be established; believe his prophets, so shall ye prosper."* So, even if there are many avenues and ways to prosper, God reveals to us a mystery that is beyond the wisdom of this world: engaging spiritual oversight.

    For instance, when Pharaoh discovered that Joseph had the ability and mandate to take spiritual and financial oversight of the land of

Egypt, he submitted to him. Can I ask you a question? Who has God sent to you as a spiritual mentor? What spiritual authority do you submit to?

Today, God has given us the fivefold ministry as a gift in the body of Christ. Ephesians 4:11-12 says, *"And he gave some, **apostles**; and some, **prophets**; and some, **evangelists**; and some, **pastors** and **teachers**; for the **perfecting of the saints**, for the work of the ministry, for the edifying of the body of Christ"* Aligning with any of these ministry offices or even all of them will guarantee your spiritual, physical and material prosperity.

Apostles are messengers in the body of Christ sent to specific groups of people. They are what we call missionaries. By giving to missions and missionaries, you can align with this ministry office and activate God's blessing on your leadership, business, or career. This is the same for the Evangelist, who is an itinerant preacher and the other ministry offices. You can align with these spiritual mentors by sowing a seed, obeying their instructions, and giving them the honor they deserve.

In the bible, there was a woman who applied honor, obedience, and seed sowing. The bible called her the Shunammite woman (2 Kings Chapter 4). She showed kindness to Prophet Elisha out of a pure heart, but was unaware that she was activating a system of alignment; *"**He that receiveth a prophet in the name of a prophet shall receive a prophet's reward;** and he that receiveth a righteous man in the name of a righteous man shall receive a righteous man's reward."* (These were the words of Jesus concerning this subject in Matthew 10:41). Because of what she did, God gave her a son after several years of bareness.

2. **Engaging the mystery of giving** – The second way to leverage on divine advantage is to engage the mystery of giving. This is what I call God's financial protocol. God has established certain laws and principles that govern and oversee specific results in life. So, if we want to produce God's results in our lives, we must engage them.

The bible says in Proverbs 11:24, *"There is that scattereth, and yet increaseth; and there is that withholdeth more than is meet, but it tendeth to poverty."* This scripture is saying that in the spiritual realm, hoarding what belongs to you doesn't make you rich. Instead, being greedy and dealing fraudulently will make you poor. On the other hand, being freehanded and generous with your finances will cause you to prosper. There are certain areas in which God has asked us to give that can unlock a consistent breakthrough in our finances.

- Give Tithes – Malachi 3:10 says, "Bring all the tithes into the storehouse, That there may be food in My house, And try Me now in this,' Says the LORD of hosts, 'If I will not open for you the windows of heaven And pour out for you such blessing That there will not be room enough to receive it."

A tithe is ten percent of your income or increase. In ancient times, God's people paid tithes of their cattle and crops. However, since everything can be monetized in the 21st century, the easiest way to pay your tithe is in cash. Many people in the church today, are confused about where to pay their tithes, but in God's Word, we see that the tithe is for God's house. This refers to your local assembly.

According to the scripture above, engaging the mystery of tithing releases God's rain of abundant provision over your storehouse, which in modern times can be your investments or bank account. Through this principle, God gives us access to an unstoppable and unlimited supply.

- Give offerings – An offering is different from your tithe. While the tithe is a demanded seed, an offering is something you give to God out of free will, from a cheerful and grateful heart. An example of this is 1 Chronicles 29:9, *"The people rejoiced over the offerings, for they had given freely and wholeheartedly to the LORD, and King David was filled with joy."*

Just like there's power in tithing, there is tremendous power for financial rewards in giving offerings. In Philippians 4:18-19 the

191

Philippian church gave an offering to God which caused Apostle Paul to reveal a certain secret: *"But I have all, and abound: I am full, having received of Epaphroditus the things which were sent from you, an odour of a sweet smell, a sacrifice acceptable, wellpleasing to God. But my God shall supply all your need according to his riches in glory by Christ Jesus."*

When you give offerings to God, He takes it upon Himself to supply everything that may be lacking in your life. This is a mystery that can end seasons of drought and lack in your family, business, career, etc.

- Give to the poor – Another mystery of giving you need to engage is giving to the poor. Proverbs 28:27 (NIV) says, **"Those who give to the poor will lack nothing**, but those who close their eyes to them receive many curses."

Just like giving offerings, this principle guarantees God's supply and blessings in your life. Because, if those who neglect the poor will be cursed, then those who take care of the less privileged will undoubtedly be blessed. Furthermore, those who engage and operate this mystery will be rewarded personally by God. Proverbs 19:17 (JUB) says, *"**He that gives unto the poor lends unto the Lord**, and he will give him his reward."*

So, beyond your income and businesses, you can connect to another stream of resources by your seed.

- Give to widows and orphans – when God accepts you as a person, He will honor and bless you. And this is the power of committing yourself to help orphans and widows. God sees these people as being unable to help themselves and is pleased with anyone who honors them. James said in James 1:27, *"Religion that God our Father accepts as pure and faultless is this: to look after orphans and widows in their distress…"*

- Give to the kingdom- although this has been mentioned earlier, I believe it needs to be emphasized. One way to excel beyond the ordinary as a leader is to seek God's kingdom with your finances. Such people are called Kingdom Financiers; men and women who fund and sponsor missions and Christian ventures that seek to expand and extend the reach of the gospel.

Moreover, God has promised people who do this, effortless financial increase and dominion. The bible says in Matthew 6:63, *"But seek ye first the kingdom of God, and his righteousness; and all these things shall be added unto you."* God promises to add to everyone who engages this spiritual mystery; all the wealth and influence the world seeks after.

3. **Engaging the mystery prayer** – The mystery of prayer is invaluable to the success of any leader. Jesus, who we've identified as the most exceptional leader of all time, effectively engaged this principle. There was a time He revealed that the influence He exercised, and the vast multitudes that followed Him were as a result of a greater Spirit-being. Really, it was His father who He prays to that gave Him such an influence and followership.

- Prayer attracts open reward from God – Matthew 6:6, "But you, when you pray, go into your room, and when you have shut your door, pray to your Father who is in the secret place; and your Father who sees in secret will reward you openly."

I call this the closet principle. Yes, there are many leadership principles and strategies in the world today, and they are all good. But this mystery is beneath the surface. It's the part of a leader's life that no one sees. God has promised to reward you openly for keeping hours of fellowship with Him; this reward encompasses every area of your life.

- Prayer connects you with the mind of God – Jeremiah 33:3, *"Call unto me, and I will answer thee, and shew thee great and mighty things, which thou knowest not."* This means as a believer; God can reveal things to you concerning your life and destiny. If you efficiently engage this mystery, you can never be disadvantaged in life.

Furthermore, the bible says the Holy Spirit will show you things to come in the future. Why would this happen? Obviously, it's because God wants you to have an advantage as a leader. He doesn't want you to run headlong into the disasters and financial crisis of the future. More accurately, He wants you to be prepared like Noah, who built an ark against the flood. Surely, in the place of prayer, you can connect with God's mind and gain access to secrets that will make you a wonder to your world.

- Prayer makes you wise - As a leader, wisdom is a necessary virtue for achieving success and fulfilling purpose. When Solomon was made the King of Israel, he knew that he needed the wisdom to lead such a great nation. And after he had gotten God's attention through sacrifice, it was in the place of prayer he requested for wisdom. In that prayer encounter, he received a transformation that made him one of the greatest Kings that ever lived. James 1:5 further reveals that wisdom comes by prayer: *"If any of you lack wisdom, let him ask of God, that giveth to all men liberally, and upbraideth not; and it shall be given him."*

- Prayer brings protection – Psalm 91:1-2 reveals the benefits of being a man or woman of prayer:

"He that dwelleth in the secret place of the Most High shall abide under the shadow of the Almighty. I will say of the Lord, He is my refuge and my fortress: my God; in him will I trust."

In times of turmoil and destruction, God will protect and secure those who sustain fellowship and communion with Him. He will keep their businesses, families, reputations, and legacies from harm.

- Prayer brings speed – Isaiah 40:31 says, *"But those who wait on the LORD Shall renew their strength; they shall mount up with wings like eagles…"* what does this mean? Well, *wait* in this text means to depend on God for something in the place of prayer. Hence, waiting on God or praying to God causes you to have results as if you literally had eagle's wings. In other words, prayer makes you strong and empowers you to go beyond the achievements of your peers. It gives you supernatural speed. When you leverage on the advantage that prayer provides, you will soar great heights and have no competitors.

4. Engaging mystery of the Word of God

- Read and study the Word for nourishment and growth - Just as natural food nourishes and keeps your physical body healthy, the Word of God nourishes and keeps your spirit healthy. It is spiritual food. Your spirit can't grow to a stage where it can accurately follow God's leading if you don't feed it. Matthew 4:4 makes this clearer, *"But He answered and said, "It is written, 'Man shall not live by bread alone, but by every word that proceeds from the mouth of God.'"*

In addition, 1 Peter 2: 2 says, "As newborn babes, desire the sincere milk of the word, that ye may grow thereby."

As a leader, you need to leverage on divine advantage in every area of your life. Therefore, you need to ensure that your spirit is sensitive enough to align with the signals of the Holy Spirit.

- Meditate on the Word for success and prosperity - Joshua 1: 8 says, "This book of the law shall not depart out of thy mouth; but thou shalt meditate therein day and night, that thou mayest observe to do according to all that is written therein: for then thou shalt make thy way prosperous, and then thou shalt have good success." Think about this for a moment. Here, God revealed to Joshua, the secret of successful leadership; it's in filling your life with God's Word because the Word of God contains the laws that guarantee success.

When you meditate on the Word, you receive inspiration and guidance. You will know what to do even in the most challenging circumstances. David said in Psalm 119:99, *"I have more understanding than all my teachers: for thy testimonies are my meditation."*

5. Obedience

- Practice the principles you've learned by personal inspiration - James 1:25 says, "But whoso looketh into the perfect law of liberty, and continueth therein, he being not a forgetful hearer, but a doer of the work, this man shall be blessed in his deed."

Contrary to what most believers think, it is those who obey God's Word and put it to practice in their daily lives that receive God's blessings in all they do. Thus, whatever you receive in your times of personal reflection and study, put them to work. Assuredly, God will bless any action you take that is in line with His principles. in essence, practicing God's Word is obeying Him, and God blesses the obedient.

- Obey your conscience – 1 Timothy 1:19 says, "Keeping faith and a good conscience, which some have rejected and suffered shipwreck in regard to their faith."

Your conscience is the voice of your born-again human spirit. When you became born-again, it became a safe and competent guide. God's spirit often leads us through our conscience. Most times, we call it intuition or inward witness. In leveraging on the divine advantage, we must be able to pick signals from the Holy Spirit in our spirit. To do this, we must keep our conscience tender by obeying that inward witness at all times. Overriding and suppressing the conscience can corrupt it. See what 1 Timothy 4:2 says, *"...by means of the hypocrisy of liars seared in their own conscience as with a branding iron..."* Here, Paul was referring to people who had corrupted their conscience and were no longer led by God.

However, in our case, we must maintain a tender and sensitive conscience by repentance and dealing honestly in all our affairs.

- Act on divine direction and command – This is another divine mystery that cannot be ignored. God enthrones men when they obey His commands. In Genesis 26:2, Isaac decided to move with his family to Egypt because there was famine where he lived, but God appeared to him and instructed him to remain in the land. What was the outcome of His obedience? **Verses 12-13** says, *"Then Isaac sowed in that land, and received in the same year an hundredfold: and the Lord blessed him. And the man waxed great, and went forward, and grew until he became very great."* In contrast, the bible tells us that Saul rejected divine instruction and was rejected by God. He was asked to wipe out the Amalekites, old and young, their wealth, and their livestock. But Saul chose to capture the King of the Amalekites and preserve the best of their livestock (1 Samuel Chapter 15).

In another instance, the King of Israel acted on the divine instruction given by Prophet Elisha and was delivered from his enemies. 2 Kings 6: 9-10 says, *"And the man of God sent unto the King of Israel, saying, Beware that thou pass not such a place; for thither the Syrians are come down. And the King of Israel sent to the place which the man of God told him and warned him of, and saved* himself there, not once nor twice."

- Give up to go up – In your walk of faith, God will ask you to make sacrifices that will open you up to realms and dimensions of greatness. When Abraham sacrificed Isaac in his heart, God promised to make him great. Genesis 22:17-18 says, *"That in blessing I will bless thee, and in multiplying I will multiply thy seed as the stars of the heaven, and as the sand which is upon the sea shore; and thy seed shall possess the gate of his enemies; And in thy seed shall all the nations of the earth be blessed; because thou hast obeyed my voice."*

FINALLY...

The Lord Jesus Christ engaged this mystery. Philippians 2: 8-10 says, *"And being found in appearance as a man,* **He humbled Himself and became obedient to the point of death, even the death of the** *cross. **Therefore God also has highly exalted Him and given Him the name which is above every name,** that at the name of Jesus every knee should bow, of those in heaven, and of those on earth, and of those under the earth."*

Jesus gave up His glory and splendor to sacrifice Himself as a peace offering for the sins of the whole world. In doing this, He activated the glory protocol. Although He humbled Himself, God highly exalted Him.

What have you been unable to sacrifice? What have you been unable to let go of? What's the sacrifice that holds the key to your greatness? You need to discover it and pay the price for greater glory. John C. Maxwell, in his book, *The 21 irrefutable laws of leadership*, said, "A leader must give up to go up." In Reality, the way to the throne is the cross.

So, can you say you are a leader who values the spiritual approach to leadership? Are you engaging any of these mysteries in your personal life? Do you have a spiritual advantage? If you do, are you leveraging on that advantage to be a better leader to your generation?

Great leaders are men and women who know that there's a God in heaven and can align with Him to display His infinite possibilities on the earth. They leverage on divine advantage!

CONCLUSION

Now that you have come this far, it is obvious that you are passionate about making every necessary adjustments and adopt styles that make for a great leader. As we have discussed, great leadership have key ingredients that you must embrace if you must become influential as a person and as a great leader.

Now that you have learnt so much, are you willing to pay the price for great leadership? Having understood the requirements for great leadership, will you embrace the leadership style of Jesus Christ? Are you ready to perform your duties in your quest to becoming a great leader? Let's see how I can make this easy for you.

- Minding your inner circle

- Minding your business

- Emulating leadership luminaries

- Becoming a person of the people

Minding your inner circle:

If you will recall, we started our discussion by underlining the need to understand how that we are first social beings that interact with other people and consequently become affected by their opinions at one point or the other. To further drive this point home, consider the kind of friends you keep and how they must have influenced you in certain ways. You have to run this diagnosis as quick as possible and take drastic action if your friends are negative influencers. They may even be neutral and sincere, yet they are not good for you. Your duty as a growing leader who would someday become great is to checkmate every negativity in your inner circle and embrace 'friends that bring security'. Avoid friends in strangers clothing and mindset. Jesus had 70 disciples, 12 in his inner circle and 3 in his innermost circle.

Minding your business

John D. Rockefeller said "Every right implies a responsibility; every opportunity, an obligation, every possession, a duty." We both agreed that great leaders are extremely dutiful and never faint hearted. With your new passion to be a great leader you must be willing to accept the responsibilities that come with it. Taking cue from Moses, we learnt how anger cost him the much anticipated Promised Land. God's judgment was indeed heartbreaking for the faithful and meek Moses but it was irrevocable. Leadership comes with great responsibilities one of which is to first understand you and your weakness; and how you are going to turn them into strengths. To whom much is given, much is expected. Are you emotionally unstable? Do you often make unwitting judgments based? Own up to it and commit it to God who blesses all men with wisdom without up braiding. Only if we do this shall we be able to lead others in the right path.

Emulating leadership luminaries

"Whatsoever was written aforetime was written for our learning..."

Romans 15:4

Do you want to great and influential like Apostle Paul? Do you think it is possible to become a prime leader like Jesus Christ? The scriptural reference above implies that we are never left helpless when it comes to learning from life itself. God has provided copious number of people and incidences that we can draw specific lifetime lessons from.

From both biblical and contemporary examples, can emulate leadership styles like that of Apostle Paul who was gifted with not just oratory skills, but innate ability to relate with his audience on an emotional level. Paul made profound statements that always left his listeners in awe. He was a great communicator. Jesus Christ was exemplified what we can call servant-leadership. Do you sometimes think you cannot become like great Christ? Now you know you can become a great communicator, positive influencer just by walking in the footsteps of these great leaders.

Becoming a person of the people

A boss has the titles, but a leader has the people. - Simon Sinek. That makes a great different between a person who gives commands and another who leads. If we desire to be endeared to our followers, we must truly be loved by them. And that love and respect must be earned. Let me show you how.

When He saw the throngs, He was moved with pity and sympathy for them, because they were bewildered (harassed and distressed and dejected and helpless), like sheep without a shepherd.

Matthew 9:36

A great leader must show empathy to his people. Empathy is characterized by not just pity, but must be complemented by love in action. Give those around you a listening ear, heart of empathy and mind that understands.

Finally, if you often have trouble with having the supports and love of your followers, your worries are now over. As long as you're going to build arsenal of virtues as recommended in this book, you have no cause for alarm. I would greatly appreciate you appreciating my efforts in putting this books together by adopting the leadership lessons that we have discussed so far. Without any iota of doubt, you're sure to attain that great leader status you have always longed for.

About The Author

*"The plan of diligent lead to profit as surely as haste leads to poverty."**(Proverbs 21:5)**

Jean Junior Gaby Doralus is a father, a strategic leader, a coach, an entrepreneur, a founder, a go-getter and a passionate follower of Jesus Christ. He's like a flower that blossoms through the climbs.

Jean Junior Gaby Doralus was born in Haiti, Port-au-Prince on November 1986. He Studied Business Management and later became the CEO and founder of 'My Dream line LLC' and 'Klere Klere SA.' He's Christian who has learnt to listen constantly to the voice and instruction of his lord- JESUS CHRIST. It was in obedience to his lord, that he shined forth as light right from his family. And illuminating other lives around him. He believes the family is the first step to an authentic and credible leadership expression. The first place to display your quality of being a great LEADER.

Jean Junior Gaby's little star seem to glow brighter than many in his youth. Since he was a kid, till now, he has always being in the front of leadership. He is a skilled communicator with the ability to convince, persuade, and influence people and lead them to a desired destination.

Also, He was once a member of world Economic Forum, Global Shapers Community, and actively involved in social-help of his community, Port-au-Prince. In January 2014, with a project he spare headed - "Botanical Eco-Technology Parc"- he helped his community at the top 5 winners for grand challenge on more than 300 city-based hubs (Global competition, socio-Economic leadership, leading by World Economic forum and sponsored by Coca-Cola's international under the then "shaping a better future.")

Jean Junior Gaby is a leader who acknowledges the importance and the value of being chosen, responsible, organize, having people following him and depending on me for growth.

The source of Jean Junior Gaby's strength and inspiration is the Holy Spirit of God, JESUS CHRIST's pattern of leadership, and the twelve apostles. All this contributed immensely to the success of the lights I am able to shine to my generation in these 13 lessons.

CPSIA information can be obtained
at www.ICGtesting.com
Printed in the USA
LVHW050740250920
667083LV00004B/239